QUESTIONS CAN'T BE STUPID ANSWERS CAN BE !!!

DR SUMIT PUNDHIR

Made with ♥ on the Notion Press Platform
www.notionpress.com

To my parents,

Who nurtured my dreams and taught me the value of perseverance.

To my beloved wife,

Whose unwavering support and love have been my guiding light.

To my sisters,

For their constant encouragement and infectious laughter.

And to my mentors, both personal and professional,

Who shaped my path and inspired me to reach for the stars.

This book is a testament to your collective wisdom, love, and faith in me.

Thank you for being the pillars of my journey.

Contents

Introductrion

In our quest for knowledge and understanding, we constantly seek answers to questions that range from the mundane to the profound. But what exactly constitutes a good question? And how can we distinguish between insightful answers and those that fall short?

This book delves deep into the art and science of questioning and answering, exploring how we can harness the power of inquiry to expand our knowledge and challenge our assumptions. Throughout human history, questions have driven progress and innovation. From ancient philosophers pondering the nature of reality to modern scientists probing the mysteries of the universe, the ability to ask probing questions has been at the heart of discovery and enlightenment. Yet in our fast-paced, information-saturated world, we often rush to answers without fully examining the questions themselves. This book aims to rekindle our appreciation for the question - to celebrate curiosity and wonder, and to hone our skills in formulating questions that lead to genuine insight. We will explore different types of questions, from the factual to the philosophical, and examine how context shapes both our inquiries and the responses they elicit.

Along the way, we'll look at how great thinkers throughout history have used questions to challenge conventional wisdom and spark new ideas but questions are only half of the equation. Equally important is our ability to critically evaluate answers and recognize flawed reasoning. We'll dissect different types of answers, from the factual to the theoretical, and develop tools for assessing their validity and usefulness. By understanding the anatomy of both insightful and misguided answers, we can become more discerning consumers of information and more effective problem-solvers.

Ultimately, this book is a guide to thinking more deeply and communicating more effectively. Whether you're a student, professional, or simply someone with an inquiring mind, the skills of asking good questions and critically evaluating answers are invaluable in navigating our complex world. By mastering the art of inquiry, we open ourselves to new perspectives, challenge our own biases, and unlock creative solutions to the challenges we face. So let us embark on this journey of exploration and discovery.

As we delve into the fascinating world of questions and answers, we'll find that while questions themselves may never be stupid, our approach to both asking and answering them can always be refined and improved. In doing so, we take an important step towards becoming more thoughtful, engaged, and enlightened individuals.

Preface

As I sit down to write this preface, I'm struck by the journey that led to the creation of this book. What began as a personal fascination with the art of questioning has blossomed into a deep exploration of how we seek and process knowledge in our rapidly changing world.

Throughout my career and personal life, I've been continually amazed by the power of a well-crafted question to unlock new insights, challenge assumptions, and drive meaningful change. Yet I've also observed how easily we can fall into the trap of accepting flawed or superficial answers, often without realizing it. Questions Can't be Stupid, Answers Can Be !!!

This book is an attempt to bridge that gap - to explore the intricate dance between questions and answers that shapes our understanding of the world around us. Within these pages, you'll find a blend of philosophical inquiry, practical advice, and real-world examples drawn from fields as diverse as science, business, education, and personal development.

My goal is not to provide all the answers, but rather to equip you with the tools to ask better questions and critically evaluate the answers you receive. Whether you're a student, a professional, or simply someone curious about the world, I hope this book will inspire you to embrace the art of questioning and approach knowledge with both skepticism and wonder.

As you embark on this journey with me, I invite you to keep an open mind, challenge your own assumptions, and never stop asking "why?" For it is in the questioning that we truly grow and learn.

Thank you for joining me on this exploration. May it spark many fruitful questions and enlightening answers in your own life.

Prologue

Questions are the keys that unlock the doors of knowledge and understanding. From our earliest moments as children asking "Why?" to our deepest philosophical inquiries as adults, questions drive our quest to make sense of ourselves and the world around us. Yet not all questions - or answers - are created equal.

In a world awash with information, misinformation, and conflicting viewpoints, the ability to ask incisive questions and critically evaluate answers has never been more crucial. This book explores the art and science of effective questioning and answering - skills that are fundamental to learning, innovation, and progress in all domains of human endeavor.

We will examine what makes a question powerful and probe the anatomy of both insightful and flawed answers. We'll explore cognitive biases and logical fallacies that can lead us astray, and develop strategies for overcoming them. Through examples spanning history, science, business, and everyday life, we'll see how asking the right questions - and knowing how to find and assess answers - can solve problems, spark creativity, and deepen our understanding.

Whether you're a student, professional, leader, or simply a curious mind, honing your questioning skills can open up new realms of possibility. And in cultivating the discernment to separate wheat from chaff when it comes to answers, you'll be better equipped to navigate our complex information landscape.

So let us embark on this journey of inquiry together. For in learning to question skillfully and answer wisely, we take a profound step toward greater knowledge, clearer thinking, and a deeper engagement with the mysteries and marvels of existence. The right question, asked in the right way, can change everything. Are you ready to start asking?

CHAPTER ONE

Universal Art of Inquiry: Questioning Across Cultures

The practice of questioning has been a fundamental aspect of human intellectual and cultural development across civilizations throughout history. From ancient philosophical traditions to modern scientific inquiry, the act of questioning has played a pivotal role in shaping our understanding of the world and ourselves. This chapter explores the historical roots, key principles, and applications of questioning traditions from various cultures around the globe, drawing on references from mythology, ancient texts, and historical accounts.

As we delve into this exploration, we will uncover how different cultures have approached the art of inquiry, the challenges they've faced, and the profound impact questioning has had on human progress. By examining these diverse traditions, we can gain valuable insights into the universal importance of questioning and its relevance in our modern world.

The Roots of Questioning in Ancient Cultures

- **Indian Subcontinent**

India has a rich intellectual tradition spanning thousands of years that has embraced the practice of questioning as a means of gaining knowledge and wisdom. From ancient Vedic texts to modern philosophical discourse, questioning has played a central role in Indian thought and culture. This section explores the historical roots, key principles, and applications of India's questioning tradition, drawing on references from mythology and ancient texts.

Historical Foundations

The tradition of questioning in Indian culture dates back to ancient times. Early examples can be found in Vedic literature, including the Upanishads, which contain philosophical dialogues exploring fundamental questions about the nature of reality, consciousness, and the self.

The Prashna Upanishad, one of the oldest Upanishadic texts, depicts students posing six great questions to a wise teacher, exemplifying the use of questioning as a learning method. This text demonstrates how questioning was seen as a path to higher knowledge and understanding.

Even the Rig Veda, one of the oldest known texts, contains hymns pondering profound cosmological questions. One famous hymn asks:

"Whence this creation has arisen. Who really knows? Is there a God? Who really knows?"

These probing questions about the origins of the universe and the nature of divinity show that even the most fundamental aspects of existence were open to inquiry in ancient Indian thought.

By embracing questioning while balancing it with respect for diverse viewpoints, India can continue to draw on its rich intellectual heritage to thrive in the modern world. As we face complex global challenges, the ability to ask probing questions and critically examine our assumptions becomes more important than ever.

The words of Rabindranath Tagore serve as a fitting conclusion to this exploration of questioning in Indian culture:

"Where the mind is without fear and the head is held high;

Where knowledge is free;

Where the world has not been broken up into fragments by narrow domestic walls;

Where words come out from the depth of truth;

Where tireless striving stretches its arms towards perfection;

Where the clear stream of reason has not lost its way into the dreary desert sand of dead habit;

Where the mind is led forward by thee into ever-widening thought and action—

Into that heaven of freedom, my Father, let my country awake."

In this vision of an awakened India, the freedom to question and pursue knowledge stands at the forefront, reminding us of the enduring value of inquiry in Indian thought and culture.

- **Ancient Greece:**

In ancient Greece, the Socratic method, developed by the philosopher Socrates, emphasized the importance of asking probing questions to stimulate critical thinking and illuminate ideas. This method of inquiry formed the basis of Western philosophical tradition and continues to influence educational practices today.

Socrates is well known for using questioning to probe the validity of an assumption, analyse the logic of an argument, and explore the unknown. Questions were a means to educate his students by drawing out their understanding of a subject and then leading them to discover a set of logical conclusions instead of lecturing them on what is true or false.

- **China:**

In Chinese philosophy, particularly in Confucianism, questioning was seen as a means of self-improvement and societal harmony. Confucius himself is quoted as saying, "He who asks a question is a fool for five minutes; he who does not ask a question remains a fool forever."

The Confucian tradition emphasized the importance of continuous learning and self-reflection, which inherently involves questioning one's own beliefs and actions. This approach to questioning was not just about acquiring knowledge, but about cultivating wisdom and moral character.

- **Mythological Examples of Questioning:**

Indian mythology is replete with examples of characters questioning established norms, authority figures, and even the gods themselves. These stories serve to illustrate the importance of inquiry in Indian culture:

Draupadi's Question: In the Mahabharata, when Draupadi is staked in a game of dice, she boldly questions her husband Yudhishthira: "As the owner of whom did you lose me?" This question challenges the very notion of a husband's authority over his wife and highlights the moral complexities of the situation.

Arjuna's Dilemma: Before the great battle of Kurukshetra, Arjuna expresses doubts and questions to Lord Krishna about the morality of fighting his own kinsmen. This dialogue forms the basis of the Bhagavad Gita, one of the most important philosophical texts in Indian tradition.

Maitreyi's Inquiry: In the Brihadaranyaka Upanishad, Maitreyi asks her husband, the sage Yajnavalkya: "My lord, if this whole earth filled with wealth were mine, would I be immortal through it?" This profound question cuts to the heart of materialism and the search for true meaning in life.

In **Greek Mythology**, Prometheus, who stole fire from the gods to give to humanity, represents the questioning of divine authority and the pursuit of knowledge. His defiance of Zeus and willingness to suffer for the sake of human progress embodies the spirit of questioning the established order.

In **Norse Mythology**, the god Odin sacrifices his eye and hangs himself from the World Tree Yggdrasil for nine days and nights to gain wisdom and knowledge of the runes, demonstrating the lengths one might go to in the pursuit of understanding.

These mythological examples demonstrate how questioning was not only accepted but often celebrated in Indian culture, even when it challenged established norms or authority figures.

- **Historical Examples of Questioning**

Throughout history, individuals who dared to question prevailing beliefs have often driven significant societal changes:

Galileo Galilei: His questioning of the geocentric model of the universe led to a revolution in our understanding of astronomy, despite facing persecution from religious authorities. Galileo's insistence on empirical evidence and mathematical proof challenged the established dogma of his time and laid the groundwork for modern scientific inquiry.

Socrates: His constant questioning of Athenian society and its values ultimately led to his execution, but his methods laid the foundation for Western philosophy. Socrates' approach of questioning everything, including his own knowledge ("I know that I know nothing"), exemplifies the power of inquiry in uncovering truth and wisdom.

Emperor Akbar: He demonstrated openness to diverse beliefs when he espoused a strong case for a new religious path Din-i Ilahi, which envisioned embracing and synthesizing the best in multitudes of religious beliefs and convictions. As a process, he advocated Rahi Aql, the path of reason, rather than blind faith, in deciding the path.

René Descartes: The French philosopher's famous statement "I think, therefore I am" came from his method of systematic doubt, where he questioned everything, he thought he knew. This approach laid the foundation for modern rationalism and scientific scepticism.

Mary Wollstonecraft: Her questioning of gender roles and the status of women in society in her work "A Vindication of the Rights of Woman" was groundbreaking for its time and laid the foundation for modern feminism.

These historical figures demonstrate how questioning established norms and beliefs can lead to profound advancements in human knowledge and social progress.

Key Principles followed across cultures while questioning:

- **Curiosity and Wonder:** Questions often arise from a sense of curiosity about the world and wonder at its mysteries. The Rig Veda's cosmological inquiries exemplify this spirit of wonder.
- **Critical Thinking:** Questioning involves applying reason and logic to examine ideas critically rather than accepting them blindly. This aligns with the Buddhist emphasis on investigation and reasoning.
- **Open-Mindedness:** Indian thought encourages considering multiple perspectives and remaining open to new ideas. Emperor Akbar exemplified this by exploring diverse religious views and advocating for the "path of reason" (Rahi Aql) in matters of faith.
- **Respectful Dialogue:** While questioning is encouraged, it is ideally done in a spirit of mutual respect and constructive dialogue rather than hostile debate.
- **Empirical Observation:** Many questioning traditions emphasize the importance of direct observation and experience. This is particularly evident in scientific inquiry and certain philosophical traditions like Buddhism.
- **Systematic Doubt:** Some traditions, like Cartesian philosophy, advocate for systematic doubt as a means of arriving at certain knowledge.
- **Ethical Consideration:** Many questioning traditions, particularly in Eastern philosophy, emphasize the ethical implications of knowledge and inquiry.

Who can be Questioned:

In modern times, there is always a debate that what and Who can be questioned but there was no such dilemma in ancient times as everyone and everything was open to be questioned. Debate was considered as the way to enhance intellect and people used to gather for witnessing debates.

Indian culture has been possibly the strongest advocate of questioning and the no one including the almighty gets immunity, all institutions and all segments can be questioning, while the intention of questioning is always the mutual growth and not to humiliate. The term "Tark-Shastra" or "Vaad-Vivad" signifies the deep roots of this practise. Some of the examples of institutions and branches of society which were often questioned were:

Philosophy and Religion:

Indian philosophical traditions like Buddhism, Jainism, and the orthodox Hindu schools all employed questioning and debate to refine their ideas. The Buddhist Councils, for example, served as platforms for healthy and non-acrimonious public discussions.

In the Jaina Sūtra 1.4.3, we find a dialogue between a Jain teacher and some sceptics of non-harm, who think that killing and eating animals is okay. The Jain asks one sceptic, "Do you find pain pleasant or unpleasant?" The answer, of course, is that it's unpleasant. Since pain is unpleasant for sceptics as well as all other living creatures, the implication is that they should not enact on other beings what they themselves find unpleasant.

Even those who believe in a God, future lives, or an immaterial self, defend their ideas through debate and reasoning, taking seriously potential challenges to their views.

In Western philosophy, the tradition of questioning is equally strong. Socrates' method of questioning to expose the weaknesses in people's beliefs has been influential for over two millennia. The scholastic tradition in medieval Europe also emphasized questioning and debate as a means of arriving at truth.

Science and Education:

The scientific method, based on questioning and empirical testing, forms the basis of modern scientific inquiry. This approach has its roots in the questioning traditions of ancient cultures but has evolved into a rigorous methodology for advancing knowledge.

In education, progressive methods emphasize inquiry-based learning to foster critical thinking skills in students. This approach draws inspiration from ancient questioning traditions like the Socratic method.

The importance of questioning in science education is highlighted by the following quote from a student: "I've been taught all my life to find the right answer, but I realize now that I need to ask the right question". This reflects a shift from rote learning to critical inquiry in modern education.

Social Reform and Governance:

Questioning of social practices has led to significant reforms throughout history, from the abolition of slavery to the push for gender equality. In India, social reformers like Raja Ram Mohan Roy questioned practices like sati, leading to its abolition.

In modern governance, mechanisms like freedom of information laws exemplify how questioning has been institutionalized to promote transparency in democracies. The Right to Information Act in India is a prime example of this.

The tradition of questioning in different cultures offers valuable lessons for cultivating wisdom, advancing knowledge, and addressing societal challenges. From the ancient Vedic seers to modern social reformers, the spirit of inquiry has been a driving force in Indian intellectual and cultural life.

Challenges to a Questioning Culture:

While questioning has a strong foundation in many cultural traditions, challenges to a questioning culture persist in many societies:

- Respect for authority figures can sometimes inhibit questioning
- Social hierarchies may limit who can engage in intellectual discourse
- Religious or political orthodoxy may resist questioning of established doctrines
- Fear of appearing ignorant or challenging the status quo can stifle inquiry
- Educational systems that prioritize rote learning over critical thinking

It's important to note that these challenges are not unique to any one culture but have been observed in various societies throughout history.

The Value of Questioning in Modern Society:

In contemporary society, the practice of questioning finds applications across various domains:

Scientific Advancement: The scientific method, based on questioning and empirical testing, continues to drive technological and medical advancements.

Critical Thinking in Education: Progressive educational methods emphasize inquiry-based learning to foster critical thinking skills in students.

Social Progress: Questioning of social norms and practices continues to drive social reform and progress.

Informed Citizenship: In democratic societies, the ability to question and critically evaluate information is crucial for informed citizenship.

Innovation in Business: Companies that encourage a culture of questioning and innovation often lead in their industries.

Personal Growth: The ability to question one's own beliefs and assumptions is crucial for personal growth and development.

Questioning: A psychological perspective

From a psychological perspective, questioning serves several important functions,

it plays a vital role in cognitive development, knowledge acquisition, emotional intelligence, creativity, memory enhancement, and metacognition from a psychological perspective.

- **Cognitive Development**

Questioning stimulates critical thinking and problem-solving skills, which are crucial for cognitive development. For example:

- Jean Piaget's theory of cognitive development emphasized how children actively construct knowledge through questioning and exploring their environment.

- The Socratic method of teaching uses probing questions to encourage students to examine their beliefs and expand their understanding.

- A 2015 study by Chin and Osborne found that students who were taught to ask higher-order questions showed improved scientific reasoning skills.

- **Knowledge Acquisition**

Questions are a primary means of acquiring new information and understanding. For instance:

- Children typically go through a "why" phase around ages 2-4, constantly asking questions to learn about their world.

- The scientific method relies on asking testable questions to gain new knowledge through experimentation.

- A 2018 study by Roelle et al. found that prompting students to generate their own questions about study material improved learning outcomes compared to just reading.

- **Emotional Intelligence**

The ability to ask appropriate questions in social situations is key for emotional intelligence:

- Psychologist Daniel Goleman highlighted "social awareness" as a core component of EI, which involves asking questions to understand others' perspectives.

- Active listening techniques emphasize asking clarifying questions to fully understand the speaker's message and emotions.

- A 2020 study by Abe et al. found that training in asking empathetic questions improved medical students' communication skills with patients.

- **Creativity**

Questioning assumptions and norms can lead to creative breakthroughs:

- Einstein's thought experiments, like imagining riding alongside a light beam, led to revolutionary theories by questioning fundamental assumptions.

- Design thinking methodology emphasizes asking "How might we...?" questions to reframe problems and generate innovative solutions.

- A 2019 study by Beaty et al. found that divergent thinking tasks involving unusual questions activated brain networks associated with creativity.

- **Memory Enhancement**

The act of questioning can reinforce memory and deepen understanding:

- The testing effect shows that retrieving information through quizzing improves long-term retention more than passive re-reading.

- Elaborative rehearsal, which involves asking questions about new information and relating it to existing knowledge, leads to better memory encoding.

- A 2016 meta-analysis by Rowland found that practice testing through questioning had large positive effects on learning outcomes across diverse contexts.

- **Metacognition**

Questioning promotes metacognition - thinking about one's own thinking processes:

- Self-questioning strategies, like "What do I already know about this topic?", help students monitor their own comprehension.

- Reflective practice in professional development often involves asking metacognitive questions to analyze one's performance and learning.

- A 2018 study by van de Pol et al. found that prompting students to ask themselves metacognitive questions improved their problem-solving abilities.

Fostering a Questioning Mindset:

Questioning can easily be misunderstood and it is very important to cultivate a culture where the mindset of questioning is been fostered well, some of the practises and techniques which have helped me and people around me are shared. Some of these may work for everyone and for others there is second reading of this book will be required.

Encourage Curiosity

Curiosity is the foundation of a questioning mindset. To foster this essential trait, we must create environments that not only allow for curiosity but actively encourage it. This begins with recognizing and rewarding curious behavior, rather than dismissing or suppressing it.

In educational settings, teachers can implement curiosity-driven learning approaches. For example, the "Genius Hour" concept, popularized by companies like Google, allows students to spend a portion of their time exploring topics that genuinely interest them. This approach has been successfully adapted in schools, with students developing projects based on their own questions and interests.

Parents can nurture curiosity at home by engaging in "wonder walks" with their children, where they explore the neighborhood and ask questions about what they observe. This simple activity can spark a lifelong love of learning and questioning.

In the workplace, leaders can foster curiosity by implementing "no-stupid-questions" policies and dedicating time in meetings for open-ended exploration of ideas. Companies like Pixar have famously used techniques like "plussing," where team members build on each other's ideas without criticism, to create an environment where curiosity thrives.

Practice Active Listening

Active listening is a crucial skill for developing a questioning mindset. It involves fully concentrating on what is being said rather than just passively hearing the message. This practice allows for more thoughtful and relevant questions to emerge.

One effective technique for active listening is the RASA method developed by Julian Treasure: Receive (pay attention to the speaker), Appreciate (make small noises like "hmm" to show engagement), Summarize (repeat back key points), and Ask (ask questions to clarify and expand understanding).

In professional settings, active listening can be practiced through techniques like "mirroring," where you repeat back what you've heard to ensure understanding. This not only improves comprehension but also naturally leads to more insightful questions.

For personal relationships, the "5-minute rule" can be effective. This involves giving your full, undivided attention to someone for five minutes, focusing solely on listening and asking follow-up questions. This practice can significantly improve communication and deepen relationships.

Challenge Assumptions

Challenging our own assumptions is a critical aspect of developing a questioning mindset. This involves regularly examining our beliefs and the basis for our opinions.

One practical method for challenging assumptions is the "Five Whys" technique, originally developed by Sakichi Toyoda for the Toyota Motor Corporation. This involves asking "why" five times to get to the root of a problem or belief. For example, if you believe you need a new car, asking "why" repeatedly might reveal that your actual need is for more reliable transportation, which could be solved in various ways.

Another effective approach is to practice "devil's advocate" thinking. This involves deliberately taking an opposing viewpoint to your own beliefs to test their validity. This can be done individually or as a group exercise in brainstorming sessions.

In academic settings, teaching critical thinking skills explicitly can help students learn to challenge assumptions. Techniques like analysing source credibility, identifying logical fallacies, and examining evidence can all contribute to a more questioning mindset.

Embrace Uncertainty

Embracing uncertainty is a key component of fostering a questioning mindset. It involves becoming comfortable with not knowing and seeing gaps in knowledge as opportunities for learning rather than threats to one's competence.

One way to cultivate this mindset is through exposure to diverse perspectives and ideas. Reading widely across different disciplines, engaging with people from various backgrounds, and traveling to new places can all help broaden one's perspective and highlight the limitations of our current knowledge.

In educational settings, teachers can model embracing uncertainty by admitting when they don't know something and demonstrating how to find answers. This shows students that it's okay not to have all the answers and that questioning is a valuable part of the learning process.

In the business world, companies can foster this mindset by encouraging experimentation and treating failures as learning opportunities. For example, Amazon's approach to "failing fast" and learning from mistakes has been key to its innovation success.

Use Open-Ended Questions

Open-ended questions are those that cannot be answered with a simple "yes" or "no." They encourage deeper thinking and more detailed responses, making them invaluable for fostering a questioning mindset.

In journalism, the "Five Ws and One H" (Who, What, When, Where, Why, and How) are classic open-ended questions that can be adapted to many situations. For example, instead of asking "Did you enjoy the movie?", one might ask "What aspects of the movie did you find most engaging?"

In educational settings, teachers can use Bloom's Taxonomy to craft questions that promote higher-order thinking. For instance, instead of asking "What happened in the story?", they might ask "How might the story have been different if it was set in a different time period?"

In personal relationships, using open-ended questions can lead to more meaningful conversations. For example, instead of asking "How was your day?", one might ask "What was the most interesting part of your day?"

Engage in Socratic Dialogue

The Socratic method, named after the ancient Greek philosopher Socrates, involves asking probing questions to stimulate critical thinking and illuminate ideas. This approach can be highly effective in fostering a questioning mindset.

In educational settings, teachers can use Socratic seminars, where students engage in collaborative dialogue about a text or topic. The teacher acts as a facilitator, asking open-ended questions to guide the discussion and encourage deeper analysis.

In professional development, Socratic questioning can be used in coaching and mentoring relationships. For example, instead of giving direct advice, a mentor might ask questions like "What do you think are the potential consequences of that decision?" or "How does this align with your long-term goals?"

In personal growth, individuals can practice self-Socratic dialogue by regularly questioning their own beliefs and decisions. This can involve asking questions like "Why do I believe this?" or "What evidence supports this view?"

Cultivate Empathy

Empathy, the ability to understand and share the feelings of another, is crucial for developing a questioning mindset that considers diverse perspectives. By cultivating empathy, we can ask more insightful and considerate questions.

One effective technique for developing empathy is perspective-taking exercises. This involves imagining oneself in another person's situation and considering their thoughts and feelings. In educational settings, this can be incorporated into literature studies or history lessons, asking students to consider events from different characters' or historical figures' perspectives.

In professional settings, empathy can be fostered through practices like job shadowing or cross-functional team projects, which allow employees to understand the challenges and perspectives of different roles within the organization.

In personal relationships, active empathetic listening can be practiced. This involves not just hearing the words someone is saying, but trying to understand the emotions and motivations behind them. This can lead to more meaningful questions and deeper understanding.

Promote Interdisciplinary Thinking

Interdisciplinary thinking involves making connections between different fields of knowledge, which can lead to novel questions and insights. Promoting this type of thinking is essential for fostering a comprehensive questioning mindset.

In educational settings, this can be achieved through integrated curricula that combine multiple subjects. For example, a project on climate change might incorporate elements of science, geography, economics, and politics, encouraging students to ask questions that span these disciplines.

In research, interdisciplinary collaboration can lead to breakthrough discoveries. For instance, the field of bioinformatics emerged from the intersection of biology and computer science, leading to new questions and methodologies in genetic research.

In business, companies can promote interdisciplinary thinking by creating cross-functional teams or hosting innovation workshops that bring together employees from different departments. This can lead to new product ideas or process improvements that wouldn't have emerged from siloed thinking.

Foster a Safe Environment

Creating a safe environment where people feel comfortable asking questions without fear of judgment is crucial for fostering a questioning mindset. This involves building a culture of psychological safety, where mistakes are seen as learning opportunities and diverse viewpoints are welcomed.

In educational settings, teachers can create this environment by responding positively to all questions, even if they seem off-topic or "silly." They can also implement practices like anonymous question boxes, where students can submit questions without fear of embarrassment.

In the workplace, leaders can foster psychological safety by admitting their own mistakes and uncertainties, and by actively soliciting input from all team members, regardless of their position in the hierarchy. Google's Project Aristotle found that psychological safety was the most important factor in effective teams.

In personal relationships, creating a safe environment for questioning involves practicing non-judgmental listening and responding to questions with openness and respect, even if you disagree with the premise.

Model Questioning Behaviour

Finally, one of the most effective ways to foster a questioning mindset is to model it yourself. This involves demonstrating the value of questioning in your own actions and decisions.

Leaders can model questioning behaviour by regularly asking for feedback and demonstrating how they use questions to make decisions. For example, a CEO might share how they questioned assumptions when developing a new business strategy.

Teachers can model questioning by thinking aloud as they work through problems, showing students how to use questions to guide their thinking. They can also demonstrate how to research answers to questions they don't know.

Parents can model questioning behaviour by expressing curiosity about the world around them and showing children how to find answers to their questions. This could involve looking up information together or designing simple experiments to test hypotheses.

By consistently demonstrating the value and process of questioning, we can inspire others to develop their own questioning mindsets, creating a culture of curiosity and continuous learning.

As we face complex global challenges in the 21st century, the ability to ask probing questions and critically examine our assumptions becomes more important than ever. By embracing a culture of inquiry while balancing it with respect for diverse viewpoints, we can draw on the rich intellectual heritage of cultures worldwide to navigate the complexities of our modern world.

The words of Indian author Anand Neelakantan serve as a fitting conclusion to this exploration of questioning across cultures:

"Parents can tell children that these stories simply exist and that it was up to them whether they want to accept them or not. There are millions of stories. They can find their own story... It is not like there is one book and if you don't believe it, you go to hell. There are millions of books. If you don't like them, create your own ideas. It's as liberal as that."

This perspective encapsulates the essence of a truly questioning mindset - one that is open to exploration, critical thinking, and the creation of new ideas. As we move forward, fostering such a mindset across cultures may be key to addressing the complex challenges of our interconnected world.

In the end, the art of questioning is not just about finding answers, but about continually expanding our understanding, challenging our assumptions, and pushing the boundaries of human knowledge. It is through this process of inquiry that we grow as individuals and as a society,

CHAPTER TWO

Questioning: The Pursuit of Knowledge

The pursuit of knowledge through questioning is a fundamental aspect of human curiosity and intellectual growth. However, as we navigate the complex landscape of inquiry, we encounter areas where questioning is encouraged, areas where it's restricted, and even domains where it might be considered taboo or dangerous. This section aims to explore the boundaries of inquiry, examining what can be questioned freely and what areas face limitations or restrictions.

The Foundations of Questioning

Questions are the building blocks of inquiry. They arise from curiosity, doubt, or the desire to understand. At their core, questions are expressions of human wonder about the world around us and our place in it.

Throughout history, the act of questioning has been both celebrated and suppressed. From ancient philosophical traditions to modern scientific inquiry, questioning has driven human progress. However, it has also faced resistance from various quarters, including religious institutions, political regimes, and social norms.

We have witnessed the references that pieces of a big knowledge jigsaw puzzle got discovered by asking the questions & pursuing them. Science, as an example, thrives on questioning. Even well-established theories are open to scrutiny and potential revision in light of new evidence.

Newtonian physics, also known as classical mechanics, was the dominant framework for understanding the physical world for over two centuries before Einstein's theories of relativity challenged and expanded upon it. Here are the key aspects of Newtonian physics and how they were questioned by relativity:

Fundamental Principles of Newtonian Physics

- **Newton's Laws of Motion**

First Law: An object remains at rest or in uniform motion in a straight line unless acted upon by an external force.

Second Law: The acceleration of an object is directly proportional to the net force acting on it and inversely proportional to its mass. This is often expressed as $F = ma$.

Third Law: For every action, there is an equal and opposite reaction.

- **Law of Universal Gravitation**

Newton proposed that two particles attract each other with a force proportional to the product of their masses and inversely proportional to the square of the distance between them.

- **Concepts of Space and Time**

In Newtonian physics, space and time were considered absolute and independent of each other. Time was thought to flow uniformly throughout the universe, and space was viewed as a fixed, immutable stage on which physical events occurred.

Limitations and Challenges to Newtonian Physics

- **Special Relativity:** Einstein's special relativity, published in 1905, introduced several concepts that contradicted Newtonian physics:
- **Constancy of Light Speed**: The speed of light is constant for all observers, regardless of their relative motion.
- **Relativity of Simultaneity**: Events that appear simultaneous to one observer may not be simultaneous to another.
- **Time Dilation**: Time passes more slowly for objects moving at high speeds relative to stationary observers.
- **Length Contraction**: Objects appear shorter in the direction of motion when traveling at high speeds.
- **Mass-Energy Equivalence**: Einstein's famous equation $E = mc^2$ showed that mass and energy are interchangeable.

Einstein's General Relativity

Einstein's general relativity, published in 1915, further expanded on the limitations of Newtonian physics:

- **Gravity as Spacetime Curvature**: Instead of a force, gravity is described as the curvature of spacetime caused by mass and energy.
- **Non-Euclidean Geometry**: The geometry of spacetime is not fixed but can be affected by the presence of matter and energy.
- **Gravitational Time Dilation**: Time passes more slowly in stronger gravitational fields.
- **Light Deflection**: Light bends as it passes through gravitational fields, a phenomenon not accounted for in Newtonian physics.

Implications and Observations

- **Mercury's Orbit**: General relativity accurately predicted the precession of Mercury's orbit, which Newtonian physics could not fully explain.
- **Gravitational Lensing**: The bending of light by massive objects, as predicted by general relativity, has been observed and is now used as a tool in astronomy.
- **GPS Technology**: The time dilation effects predicted by both special and general relativity must be accounted for in GPS satellites to maintain accuracy.
- **Black Holes and Gravitational Waves**: These phenomena, predicted by general relativity, have been observed and studied, further validating Einstein's theories.

While Einstein's theories of relativity have superseded Newtonian physics in explaining certain phenomena, especially at very high speeds or in strong gravitational fields, Newtonian physics remains highly accurate and useful for most everyday calculations and engineering applications. The transition from Newtonian physics to relativity represents a profound shift in our understanding of the fundamental nature of space, time, and gravity.

If this science stuff played hard on you then the following social and philosophical examples are going to take us outside laboratory and give us the view of world around us.

LGBTQ+ movement for their rights is all about asking the right questions towards society and getting the due response. Even the whole section of ontological section of philosophy focuses on questioning the nature of reality or epistemology questions the nature of knowledge itself.

Historically the concept of questioning has cases of repercussions as well but if the convention needs to be changed and a new idea or way of life has to exist then questions are here to stay & while everything is open for questions, there are still some aspects which are tough to negotiate while questioning & while some these topics can be personal belief system like Religion, Cultural and ethnic identity or ethical boundaries in science like Animal Testing or Human Engineering, the discussion on how to question in order to find a right answer will be discussed in detail towards later part of this book. Towards the conclusion of this chapter, we will also discuss on the strategy of effective questioning

Strategy for Effective Questioning

Developing Critical Thinking Skills

"**Logical Reasoning**" is a fundamental component of effective questioning. It involves the ability to identify logical fallacies, construct sound arguments, and analyse the validity of claims. This skill enables individuals to dissect complex issues, recognize patterns, and draw well-founded conclusions. Developing logical reasoning often requires practice in formal and informal logic, as well as exposure to various forms of argumentation.

"**Information Literacy**" is crucial in today's information-rich environment. It encompasses the ability to locate, evaluate, and use information effectively. This skill involves understanding the credibility of different sources, recognizing bias, and distinguishing between fact and opinion. Information literacy also includes the capacity to synthesize information from multiple sources and apply it to form well-reasoned questions and arguments.

"**Metacognition**", or thinking about one's own thinking, is essential for effective questioning. It involves self-reflection on cognitive processes, biases, and assumptions. By developing metacognitive skills, individuals can become more aware of their own thought patterns, identify gaps in their understanding, and adjust their questioning strategies accordingly. This self-awareness can lead to more insightful and probing questions.

Cultivating Open-Mindedness

"**Exposure to Diverse Perspectives**" broadens one's understanding and challenges preconceived notions. This involves actively seeking out viewpoints that differ from one's own, whether through reading diverse literature, engaging in cross-cultural experiences, or participating in discussions with people from various backgrounds. Such exposure can lead to more nuanced and comprehensive questioning.

"**Practicing Empathy**" is about trying to understand others' points of view, even when they differ significantly from one's own. This skill involves active listening, suspending judgment, and attempting to see situations from multiple angles. Empathy in questioning allows for more respectful and productive dialogues, as it demonstrates a genuine interest in understanding rather than merely challenging or refuting.

"**Embracing Uncertainty**" is a key aspect of open-minded questioning. It involves being comfortable with ambiguity and unanswered questions. This mindset allows for more exploratory and speculative questioning, rather than always seeking definitive answers. Embracing uncertainty can lead to more creative and innovative thinking, as it encourages considering multiple possibilities and hypothetical scenarios.

Ethical Considerations in Questioning

"**Respect for Others**" is paramount in ethical questioning. While the right to question is fundamental, it must be balanced with respect for others' beliefs, cultures, and sensitivities. This involves considering the context and potential impact of questions, especially when dealing with sensitive or controversial topics. Respectful questioning seeks to understand rather than to judge or belittle.

"**Consideration of Consequences**" involves weighing the potential impacts of questioning sensitive topics. This ethical aspect requires foresight and responsibility, recognizing that certain questions or the manner in which they are asked can have significant personal, social, or political ramifications. It's about striking a balance between the pursuit of knowledge and the potential for harm or distress.

"**Intellectual Honesty**" is about maintaining integrity in the pursuit of knowledge. This involves being truthful about one's own knowledge limitations, admitting mistakes, and being willing to change one's mind in light of new evidence. Intellectual honesty also means avoiding manipulation of facts or selective use of information to support predetermined conclusions.

Effective Communication of Questions

"**Framing Questions Constructively**" is about phrasing inquiries in a non-confrontational and productive manner. This involves using neutral language, avoiding loaded terms, and structuring questions to encourage thoughtful responses rather than defensive reactions. Constructive framing can lead to more open and fruitful discussions.

"**Active Listening**" is a critical skill in effective questioning. It involves fully concentrating on what is being said, understanding the message, and responding thoughtfully. Active listening allows for more relevant follow-up questions and demonstrates respect for the person being questioned. It also helps in identifying nuances and underlying issues that may not be immediately apparent.

"**Creating Safe Spaces,** as mentioned earlier as well, for Dialogue" is about fostering environments where questioning is encouraged and valued. This involves establishing ground rules for respectful communication, acknowledging the value of diverse perspectives, and creating an atmosphere where people feel comfortable expressing doubts or asking for clarification. Safe spaces promote more honest and in-depth questioning and discussion.

The act of questioning is a powerful tool for advancing knowledge and understanding. While there are areas where questioning faces limitations or resistance, the overall trend in many societies is towards greater openness to inquiry. As we navigate the complex landscape of what can and cannot be questioned, it's crucial to balance the pursuit of knowledge with ethical considerations and respect for diverse perspectives.

The ability to ask good questions – and to know when and how to ask them – is a vital skill in our rapidly changing world. By fostering a culture of thoughtful, responsible questioning, we can continue to push the boundaries of human knowledge while respecting the sensitivities and limitations that exist in various domains.

As we look to the future, the nature of questioning itself may evolve with technological advancements and shifting social norms. However, the fundamental human drive to understand and explore will likely continue to fuel our quest for knowledge through questioning.

CHAPTER THREE

Art of Asking: Right Question Lead to the Right Answer

The Power of Questions

Questions are the keys that unlock the doors of knowledge, understanding, and innovation. They are the driving force behind human progress, scientific discoveries, and personal growth. The statement "The right question will get the right answer" encapsulates a profound truth about the nature of inquiry and problem-solving.

In this section, we will explore the multifaceted world of questioning, examining how the art of asking the right questions can lead to transformative insights and solutions across various domains of human endeavour. We will delve into the philosophy and psychology of questioning, analyse different types of questions and their purposes, and investigate the role of questions in fields ranging from science to personal development.

By understanding the power of questions and honing our ability to ask the right ones, we can unlock new realms of possibility and navigate the complexities of our world with greater clarity and purpose.

The Philosophy of Questioning

The act of questioning has been a cornerstone of philosophical inquiry since ancient times. Socrates, the Greek philosopher, famously used questions as a method of eliciting truth and exposing the limitations of presumed knowledge. His approach, known as the Socratic method, involves asking probing questions to stimulate critical thinking and illuminate ideas.

In Eastern philosophy, questioning also plays a crucial role. Zen Buddhism, for instance, uses koans - paradoxical questions or statements - to provoke "great doubt" and ultimately lead to enlightenment. The Indian philosophical tradition, too, has a rich history of questioning, as evidenced in texts like the Upanishads, which often take the form of dialogues between teachers and students.

Modern philosophers have continued to emphasize the importance of questioning. Ludwig Wittgenstein argued that many philosophical problems arise from asking the wrong questions or misunderstanding the nature of language. He famously stated, "The real discovery is the one that makes me capable of stopping doing philosophy when I want to. The one that gives philosophy peace, so that it is no longer tormented by questions which bring itself into question."

The philosophy of science, as articulated by thinkers like Karl Popper, emphasizes the role of questioning in the form of falsifiable hypotheses. According to this view, scientific progress is made not by proving theories correct, but by asking questions that could potentially prove them wrong.

The Psychology Behind Effective Questioning

From a psychological perspective, questioning serves several crucial functions in cognitive development and information processing. Developmental psychologists like Jean Piaget have shown that children's ability to ask questions is closely tied to their cognitive growth and understanding of the world.

Questions play a vital role in memory and learning. The generation effect, a phenomenon in cognitive psychology, suggests that information is better remembered when it is actively generated (e.g., by answering questions) rather than passively read or heard.

Moreover, the act of questioning can have significant effects on motivation and engagement. Self-determination theory, developed by psychologists Edward Deci and Richard Ryan, suggests that autonomy - which includes the ability to ask questions and seek answers - is a key factor in intrinsic motivation.

The concept of metacognition - thinking about one's own thinking - is closely tied to the ability to ask effective questions. By questioning our own thought processes and assumptions, we can improve our critical thinking skills and decision-making abilities.

Types of Questions and Their Purposes

Questions are fundamental tools in human communication, learning, and critical thinking. They serve as gateways to knowledge, understanding, and personal growth. In various contexts - from casual conversations to formal interviews, classroom discussions to scientific inquiries - different types of questions play crucial roles in shaping the depth and direction of our interactions and thought processes. Understanding the various types of questions and their specific purposes is essential for effective communication, education, and problem-solving. This exploration delves into the diverse landscape of question types, examining how each category serves unique functions in eliciting information, stimulating thought, and fostering deeper understanding. By recognizing and skillfully employing these different question types, we can enhance our ability to gather information, promote learning, and engage in meaningful dialogue across various personal, professional, and academic settings.

Open-ended vs. Closed-ended Questions

Open-ended questions invite respondents to provide detailed, expansive answers. They often begin with words like "how," "why," or "describe," encouraging exploration and elaboration. For example, "How did you feel about the movie?" allows for a wide range of responses. These questions are particularly useful in qualitative research, therapy sessions, and creative brainstorming.

Closed-ended questions, on the other hand, typically elicit short, specific answers. They often require a simple "yes" or "no" response or a selection from predetermined options. For instance, "Did you enjoy the movie?" limits the response to affirmation or negation. These questions are valuable in surveys, quick assessments, and when gathering quantifiable data.

Factual vs. Conceptual Questions

Factual questions seek specific, concrete information. They often begin with "who," "what," "when," or "where." For example, "What year did World War II end?" requires a precise, factual answer. These questions are essential in assessing knowledge retention and gathering objective information.

Conceptual questions, conversely, probe understanding of ideas, theories, and relationships. They often start with "why" or "how" and require deeper thinking. For instance, "How did the Industrial Revolution impact social structures?" encourages analysis and synthesis of information. These questions are crucial in academic settings and for assessing higher-order thinking skills.

Convergent vs. Divergent Questions

Convergent questions aim for a single, correct answer. They are often used in standardized tests and fact-checking scenarios. For example, "What is the capital of France?" has only one correct response. These questions are useful for assessing specific knowledge and ensuring clarity in communication.

Divergent questions, in contrast, encourage multiple perspectives and creative thinking. They often have no single correct answer and are used to stimulate discussion and innovation. For instance, "How might we solve the problem of plastic pollution?" invites various approaches and ideas. These questions are valuable in brainstorming sessions, creative writing, and problem-solving exercises.

Probing Questions

Probing questions are follow-up inquiries that seek clarification or deeper exploration of a topic. They are often used in interviews, counseling sessions, and classroom discussions to encourage elaboration and critical thinking. For example, after an initial response, one might ask, "Can you tell me more about that?" or "What led you to that conclusion?" These questions help uncover underlying thoughts, motivations, and reasoning.

Hypothetical Questions

Hypothetical questions explore potential scenarios and their implications. They often begin with phrases like "What if" or "Imagine that." For instance, "What would you do if you won the lottery?" These questions are useful in strategic planning, creative problem-solving, and assessing decision-making skills. They encourage imaginative thinking and can reveal values and priorities.

Reflective Questions

Reflective questions encourage self-examination and metacognition - thinking about one’s own thought processes. They prompt individuals to consider their experiences, beliefs, and learning processes. Examples include "What did you learn from this experience?" or "How has your perspective changed?" These questions are valuable in personal development, education, and professional growth, fostering self-awareness and continuous improvement.

Leading Questions

Leading questions are designed to suggest a particular answer, often used in persuasion or manipulation. They can be phrased to encourage a specific response, such as "Don't you agree that this is the best option?" While these questions can be effective in sales and marketing, they are generally discouraged in objective research, legal proceedings, and unbiased information gathering due to their potential to skew responses.

Understanding these different types of questions and their purposes is crucial for asking the right question in any given situation. Just by reading this book will not make you expert on these questions as these are traits which needs to be practised over a period of time to gain expertise but once you get command on these then there will not be any unanswered questions around you.

The Art of Formulating the Right Question

The art of formulating the right question is a fundamental skill that underpins effective communication, critical thinking, and problem-solving across all domains of human endeavour. From scientific research to business strategy, from journalism to education, the ability to ask insightful and purposeful questions can be the key that unlocks new knowledge, drives innovation, and fosters deeper understanding. In an era of information overload, where answers are often readily available at our fingertips, the true challenge lies in asking the questions that matter most. This section delves into the nuanced craft of question formulation, exploring the principles, techniques, and considerations that transform ordinary inquiries into powerful tools for discovery and insight. By mastering this art, individuals can enhance their critical thinking skills, improve decision-making processes, and cultivate more meaningful and productive dialogues in both personal and professional spheres. As we navigate through the complexities of the modern world, the capacity to ask the right questions at the right time becomes not just a valuable skill, but an essential compass for navigating the vast seas of information and possibility that surround us.

Clarity: The Foundation of Effective Questions

Clarity is paramount when formulating questions. A clear question leaves no room for misinterpretation and ensures that the respondent understands exactly what information is being sought.

Principles of Clear Questions:

- Use simple, straightforward language
- Avoid jargon unless necessary for the context
- Break complex inquiries into smaller, more manageable questions
- Define any terms that might be ambiguous

Examples:

Unclear: "What do you think about the current situation?"

Clear: "How do you feel about the recent changes in our company's work-from-home policy?"

Unclear: "Can you tell me about your experience?"

Clear: "Could you describe your experience using our new software over the past month?"

Techniques for Improving Clarity:

1. Read your question aloud to check for natural flow
2. Ask a colleague to review your questions for clarity
3. Consider the background knowledge of your audience
4. Use concrete examples when necessary to illustrate your point

Relevance: Aligning Questions with Objectives

Relevant questions are directly related to the information you seek or the problem you're trying to solve. They keep discussions focused and productive.

Ensuring Relevance:

- Clearly define your objectives before formulating questions
- Consider how each question contributes to your overall goal
- Avoid tangential or overly broad questions that may lead off-topic

Examples:

Irrelevant: "What's your favorite color?" (when interviewing for a technical position)

Relevant: "Can you describe a challenging technical problem you've solved recently?"

Techniques for Maintaining Relevance:

1. Create a question map linking each question to your objectives
2. Regularly refer back to your main goals during the questioning process
3. Be prepared to redirect conversations if they stray from the relevant topics

Open-endedness: Inviting Elaboration and Exploration

Open-ended questions invite detailed responses and encourage the exploration of ideas. They are particularly useful when seeking diverse perspectives or in-depth information.

Characteristics of Open-ended Questions:

- Cannot be answered with a simple "yes" or "no"
- Often begin with words like "how," "why," or "describe"
- Allow for a range of possible responses

Examples:

Closed: "Did you enjoy the conference?"

Open-ended: "What aspects of the conference did you find most valuable and why?"

Techniques for Crafting Open-ended Questions:

1. Start with "What," "How," "Why," or "Describe"
2. Ask for examples or elaborations
3. Invite comparisons or contrasts
4. Encourage storytelling or scenario descriptions

Neutrality: Avoiding Bias in Questions

Neutral questions are free from bias and don't suggest a particular answer. They are essential for gathering unbiased information and opinions.

Principles of Neutral Questions:

- Avoid leading language that suggests a "correct" answer
- Present all options equally when offering choices
- Use neutral tone and phrasing

Examples:

Biased: "Don't you think our new policy is great?"

Neutral: "What are your thoughts on our new policy?"

Techniques for Ensuring Neutrality:

1. Review questions for words with positive or negative connotations
2. Present multiple viewpoints when discussing controversial topics
3. Use balanced language when describing options or scenarios
4. Avoid assumptions about the respondent's opinions or experiences

Specificity: Balancing Detail and Breadth

Specific questions target precise information but should not be so narrow that they miss important related details. The right level of specificity depends on your objectives and the context of the inquiry.

Balancing Specificity:

- Be specific enough to get the information you need
- Allow room for related information that may be valuable
- Consider follow-up questions to drill down into details

Examples:

Too Vague: "What do you think about our products?"

Too Specific: "What do you think about the shade of blue used in our logo?"

Balanced: "Which features of our product line do you find most useful and why?"

Techniques for Achieving the Right Specificity:

1. Start with broader questions and narrow down based on responses
2. Use qualifiers to focus questions (e.g., "In the past month...")
3. Provide context when asking about specific details
4. Allow for "other" responses to capture unanticipated information

Sequencing: The Order of Questions Matters

The sequence of questions can significantly impact the quality and depth of responses. Thoughtful sequencing can build rapport, establish context, and lead to more insightful answers.

Principles of Question Sequencing:

- Start with easier, less sensitive questions to build rapport
- Move from general to specific inquiries
- Group related questions together
- End with more challenging or sensitive questions

Example:

1. "How long have you been using our product?"
2. "What initially attracted you to our product?"
3. "Which features do you use most frequently?"
4. "Can you describe any challenges you've encountered while using the product?"
5. "How does our product compare to others you've used?"

Techniques for Effective Sequencing:

1. Create a logical flow that builds on previous questions
2. Use transitional phrases to connect different topics
3. Be prepared to adjust the sequence based on responses
4. Consider the emotional impact of questions and sequence accordingly

Empathy: Considering the Respondent's Perspective

Empathetic questioning considers the perspective, knowledge, and comfort level of the person being asked. It helps build rapport and can lead to more honest and detailed responses.

Principles of Empathetic Questioning:

- Consider the respondent's background and expertise
- Be sensitive to potentially uncomfortable topics
- Frame questions in a way that relates to the respondent's experiences

Examples:

Less Empathetic: "Why haven't you implemented the new system yet?"

More Empathetic: "What challenges have you encountered in implementing the new system?"

Techniques for Enhancing Empathy in Questions:

1. Research your audience before formulating questions
2. Use language and examples that resonate with the respondent
3. Offer context or explanations for complex topics
4. Provide options for respondents to decline answering sensitive questions

Curiosity: Driving Questions with Genuine Interest

Genuine curiosity often leads to more insightful and unexpected answers. Curious questions can uncover new perspectives and lead conversations in productive directions.

Cultivating Curiosity in Questions:

- Approach topics with an open mind
- Be willing to challenge your own assumptions
- Show interest in the respondent's unique perspective

Examples:

Standard: "What are your job responsibilities?"

Curious: "What aspects of your work do you find most intriguing or challenging?"

Techniques for Fostering Curiosity:

1. Practice active listening and ask follow-up questions based on responses
2. Explore "what if" scenarios to encourage creative thinking
3. Ask about personal experiences related to the topic
4. Invite respondents to share their own questions or areas of curiosity

Probing: Digging Deeper for Insights

Probing questions follow up on initial responses to gain deeper understanding or clarification. They are essential for uncovering underlying motivations, beliefs, and experiences.

Types of Probing Questions:

- Clarification probes: "Can you explain what you mean by...?"
- Elaboration probes: "Tell me more about..."
- Example probes: "Can you give me a specific example of...?"
- Evidence probes: "What leads you to that conclusion?"

Techniques for Effective Probing:

1. Listen carefully to initial responses and identify areas for deeper exploration

2. Use silence effectively to encourage further elaboration

3. Reflect back key points to confirm understanding before probing further

4. Be prepared with follow-up questions based on potential responses

Hypothetical Questions: Exploring Possibilities

Hypothetical questions invite respondents to consider scenarios or possibilities beyond their current experience. They can be valuable for strategic planning, problem-solving, and understanding decision-making processes.

Crafting Effective Hypothetical Questions:

- Create realistic and relevant scenarios
- Provide enough context for the respondent to engage with the hypothetical situation
- Use hypotheticals to explore both positive and negative possibilities

Examples:

"If our main competitor were to lower their prices by 20%, how do you think we should respond?"

"Imagine you had unlimited resources to improve our product. What changes would you make and why?"

Techniques for Using Hypothetical Questions:

1. Use "what if" scenarios to explore potential future situations

2. Encourage respondents to think beyond current constraints

3. Use hypotheticals to understand priorities and decision-making criteria

4. Follow up hypothetical questions with probes about reasoning and implications

Reflective Questions: Encouraging Self-Analysis

Reflective questions prompt respondents to examine their own thoughts, feelings, and experiences. They can lead to deeper insights and self-awareness.

Characteristics of Reflective Questions:

- Encourage introspection and self-evaluation
- Often focus on personal experiences, beliefs, or decision-making processes
- Can reveal underlying motivations and values

Examples:

"Looking back on the project, what would you do differently if you could start over?"

"How has your perspective on this issue changed over time?"

Techniques for Crafting Reflective Questions:

1. Use phrases like "looking back," "in hindsight," or "upon reflection"
2. Ask about lessons learned or personal growth
3. Encourage comparisons between past and present perspectives
4. Invite respondents to consider the impact of their actions or decisions

Quantitative vs. Qualitative Questions

Understanding when to use quantitative (numerical) versus qualitative (descriptive) questions is crucial for gathering the right type of information.

Quantitative Questions:

- Seek numerical or categorical data
- Often used for statistical analysis
- Examples: rating scales, multiple choice, yes/no questions

Qualitative Questions:

- Seek descriptive, non-numerical responses
- Often used for understanding experiences, opinions, and motivations
- Examples: open-ended questions, storytelling prompts

Techniques for Balancing Quantitative and Qualitative Questions:

1. Use quantitative questions for benchmarking and tracking trends
2. Follow up quantitative questions with qualitative ones to understand the "why" behind the numbers
3. Consider mixed-method approaches that combine both types of questions
4. Choose the question type based on your research objectives and analysis plans

Mastering the art of formulating the right question is a powerful skill that can enhance communication, decision-making, and problem-solving across various domains. By applying the principles and techniques discussed in this section, you can craft questions that are clear, relevant, and effective in eliciting the information you need. Remember that questioning is an iterative process – continually refine your approach based on the responses you receive and the evolving nature of your inquiry. With practice and reflection, you can develop a questioning style that leads to deeper understanding, more productive conversations, and better outcomes in both personal and professional contexts.

Common Pitfalls in Questioning

Effective questioning is a crucial skill in various fields, from journalism and scientific research to business management and education. However, even experienced professionals can fall into common traps that compromise the quality of information gathered. This chapter explores the most prevalent pitfalls in questioning techniques, their potential consequences, and strategies to avoid them. By understanding these common mistakes, we can enhance our ability to gather accurate, meaningful information and foster productive dialogues.

Asking Too Many Questions at Once

One of the most common mistakes in questioning is overwhelming the respondent with multiple inquiries simultaneously. This approach, often stemming from enthusiasm or a desire for efficiency, can lead to several problems.

The Problem:

When faced with multiple questions at once, respondents may:

- Feel overwhelmed and unsure where to begin
- Forget parts of the question, leading to incomplete answers
- Focus on the last or most memorable part of the multi-part question
- Provide superficial answers to each part rather than in-depth responses

Examples:

Poor: "What's your background in marketing, how do you approach social media campaigns, and what metrics do you use to measure success?"

Better: "Could you tell me about your background in marketing?" (Followed by subsequent questions based on the response)

Consequences:

- Incomplete or superficial information
- Missed opportunities for follow-up questions
- Difficulty in analyzing responses due to mixed information

Strategies to Avoid This Pitfall:

1. Prioritize your questions: Determine the most critical information you need and ask about that first.

2. Use a funnel approach: Start with broader questions and narrow down based on responses.

3. Practice active listening: Allow each answer to inform your next question.

4. Create a structured question flow: Organize your questions logically, moving from one topic to the next.

Case Study: Job Interview Scenario

One of my earlier hiring managers used to bombard candidates with questions like in one case while interviewing a candidate for a marketing position, he asked, "Can you tell me about your education, your experience with digital marketing, and your biggest professional achievement?" The candidate, feeling overwhelmed, focused primarily on their education, briefly mentioned digital marketing experience, and forgot to address their biggest achievement. This resulted in an incomplete picture of the candidate's qualifications.

By instead asking these questions separately and allowing time for detailed responses to each, the interviewer would have gained a more comprehensive understanding of the candidate's background and capabilities.

Asking Yes/No Questions When More Information is Needed

Closed-ended questions, particularly yes/no questions, can be useful for gathering specific, factual information quickly. However, they often fall short when deeper insights or explanations are required.

The Problem:

Yes/no questions:

- Limit the depth and breadth of responses
- May oversimplify complex issues
- Can lead to assumptions based on limited information
- Miss opportunities for nuanced understanding

Examples:

Limited: "Do you like your job?"

Better: "How do you feel about your current role, and what aspects do you find most satisfying or challenging?"

Consequences:

- Superficial understanding of situations or opinions
- Missed opportunities for valuable insights
- Potential for misinterpretation due to lack of context
- Reduced engagement from respondents

Strategies to Avoid This Pitfall:

1. Use open-ended questions: Start questions with "how," "why," or "what" to encourage elaboration.

2. Follow up yes/no questions: If a closed-ended question is necessary, follow it with an open-ended probe.

3. Encourage storytelling: Ask for specific examples or experiences.

4. Use scaling questions: Instead of yes/no, use a scale (e.g., 1-10) and ask for explanations.

Case Study: Customer Satisfaction Survey or NPS Survey

When we conducted our first NPS Survey, we used primarily yes/no questions, such as "Was our product easy to use?" and "Did our customer service meet your expectations?" While the results showed high satisfaction rates, we company gained little insight into why customers were satisfied or what specific aspects of their product and service were most valued.

By reformulating these questions to be open-ended, such as "How would you describe your experience using our product?" and "In what ways did our customer service meet or fall short of your expectations?", we could have gathered rich, qualitative data to inform product improvements and service enhancements.

Using Leading Questions

Leading questions are those that suggest or encourage a particular answer. While sometimes used intentionally in legal or sales contexts, they are generally problematic in research, interviews, and objective information gathering.

The Problem:

Leading questions:

- Introduce bias into responses
- Can manipulate or pressure respondents
- May reflect the questioner's assumptions or preferences
- Reduce the authenticity and reliability of the information gathered

Examples:

Leading: "Don't you agree that our new policy is beneficial?"

Neutral: "What are your thoughts on the new policy?"

Consequences:

- Biased or inaccurate data
- Reduced credibility of research or interviews
- Potential ethical concerns, especially in legal or journalistic contexts
- Missed opportunities for genuine insights

Strategies to Avoid This Pitfall:

1. Use neutral language: Avoid words that suggest a preferred answer.

2. Present balanced options: If offering choices, ensure they cover a range of possibilities.

3. Ask for specific experiences: Instead of opinions, ask about concrete events or examples.

4. Review questions for bias: Have colleagues or neutral parties review your questions.

Case Study: Market Research for a New Product Launch

During one of my previous assignments, we were developing a new smartphone app for product selection & installation. To get the context & gauge potential user interest we conducted a focus group survey. The moderator asked questions like, "How excited are you about using our innovative new app?" and "Don't you think this app would make your life easier?" Participants, influenced by the positive framing, provided overwhelmingly positive feedback.

However, when the app launched, user adoption and satisfaction were much lower than anticipated. A post-launch analysis revealed that the leading questions in the focus groups had masked genuine concerns and use cases that weren't addressed in the final product.

By using neutral questions such as "How would you describe your initial reaction to this app concept?" and "In what ways, if any, do you think this app might affect your existing selection process?", the company could have gathered more authentic feedback, leading to a product better aligned with user needs and expectations.

Asking Vague or Ambiguous Questions

Vague or ambiguous questions can lead to confusion, irrelevant answers, and misinterpretation of data. Clarity in questioning is essential for obtaining accurate and useful information.

The Problem:

Vague or ambiguous questions:

- Can be interpreted differently by different respondents
- May lead to answers that don't address the intended topic
- Require additional clarification, wasting time and potentially frustrating respondents
- Can result in data that is difficult to analyze or compare

Examples:

Vague: "What do you think about the current situation?"

Specific: "How has the recent change in company policy affected your daily work routine?"

Consequences:

- Inconsistent or irrelevant responses
- Difficulty in analyzing or comparing data
- Increased time spent on clarification and follow-up
- Potential for misunderstanding or misinterpretation of results

Strategies to Avoid This Pitfall:

1. Be specific: Clearly define the subject, context, and timeframe of your question.
2. Avoid jargon or complex language: Use simple, clear terms that all respondents will understand.
3. Provide context: If necessary, offer a brief explanation before asking the question.
4. Test your questions: Pilot your questions with a small group to identify any ambiguities.

Case Study: Employee Satisfaction Survey

While working for a large multinational company, I was part of an annual employee satisfaction survey that included the question, "How do you feel about your work environment?" Responses varied widely, with some employees discussing physical office conditions, others focusing on team dynamics, and some addressing work-life balance. The ambiguity of the question made it difficult for us to identify specific areas for improvement.

By breaking this vague question into more specific inquiries, such as "How would you rate the physical comfort of your workspace on a scale of 1-10?", "How would you describe the collaborative atmosphere within your team?", and "To what extent does your current role allow for a satisfactory work-life balance?", the company could have gathered more actionable data to address specific aspects of employee satisfaction.

Failing to Listen to the Answers

Active listening is a crucial component of effective questioning. When interviewers or researchers are too focused on their next question or preconceived notions, they may miss valuable information in the responses.

The Problem:

Failing to listen attentively:

- Misses opportunities for insightful follow-up questions
- Can lead to repetitive or irrelevant questions
- Diminishes the quality of the interaction and rapport with the respondent
- May result in overlooking important details or nuances

Consequences:

- Incomplete or superficial understanding of the topic
- Missed opportunities for deeper insights
- Potential frustration or disengagement from respondents
- Reduced effectiveness of the overall questioning process

Strategies to Improve Listening:

1. Practice active listening: Focus fully on the respondent, avoiding distractions.
2. Take notes: Jot down key points to help maintain focus and inform follow-up questions.
3. Pause before responding: Allow time to process the answer before moving to the next question.
4. Reflect and summarize: Periodically summarize what you've heard to ensure understanding.

Case Study: Investigative Journalism

During the discussion with a whistleblower about misconduct by his team member, the team was so focused on covering all the points in her prepared question list (Which was focusing only on that one episode) that we failed to notice when the interviewee hinted at a much bigger issue involving the ethical behavior of the team leader. By sticking rigidly to the script and not listening attentively, we missed a bigger issue however, the same was captured during a second level discussion but by that time we lost 16 weeks and the ethical concern must have impacted many team members during that period.

If we would have practiced active listening, we could have picked up on the subtle cues and asked probing follow-up questions, potentially uncovering a more significant issue than originally anticipated.

Asking Questions with Obvious Answers

Asking questions with obvious or easily accessible answers can be perceived as a waste of time or even insulting to the respondent. It may also indicate a lack of preparation or engagement from the questioner.

The Problem:

Questions with obvious answers:

- Can come across as condescending or unprofessional
- Waste valuable time that could be spent on more insightful inquiries
- May reduce the respondent's engagement or willingness to provide thoughtful answers
- Can undermine the credibility of the questioner

Examples:

Obvious: "Do you think customer satisfaction is important for a business?"

Better: "What specific strategies have you found most effective in improving customer satisfaction in your industry?"

Consequences:

- Reduced quality of interaction and rapport
- Missed opportunities for gathering valuable insights
- Potential disengagement or frustration from respondents
- Diminished credibility of the researcher or interviewer

Strategies to Avoid This Pitfall:

1. Do your homework: Research the topic and the respondent beforehand.
2. Focus on specific experiences or insights: Ask about personal experiences or unique perspectives rather than general knowledge.
3. Use hypothetical scenarios: Present complex or nuanced situations to elicit thoughtful responses.
4. Ask for examples or elaboration: Even if a concept seems obvious, asking for specific examples can yield valuable insights.

Case Study: Executive Interview

Once the CEO of Global Electrical Company was interviewed for a video interview at exhibition stall and he started the interview by asking, "Is wired technology important in today's world?" The CEO, taken aback by the simplicity of the question, provided a brief, unenthusiastic response. This set a poor tone for the rest of the interview, with the CEO becoming less engaged and offering less insightful answers to subsequent questions.

If the reporter had instead asked a more nuanced question like, "How do you see the role of wired and wireless technology evolving in your industry over the next decade, and what unique challenges or opportunities does this present for your company?", it would have demonstrated better preparation and likely elicited a more thoughtful and informative response from the CEO.

Failing to Follow Up

Effective questioning often requires going beyond the initial response to probe deeper or clarify points. Failing to follow up on interesting or unclear answers can result in missed opportunities for valuable insights.

The Problem:

Lack of follow-up:

- Leaves potentially important information unexplored
- Can result in superficial understanding of complex topics
- Misses opportunities to clarify ambiguous or vague responses
- May lead to incorrect assumptions or interpretations

Consequences:

- Incomplete or shallow data collection
- Missed opportunities for deeper insights or unexpected discoveries
- Potential misunderstanding or misinterpretation of responses
- Reduced overall quality and depth of the information gathered

Strategies for Effective Follow-Up:

1. Use probing questions: Ask "Why?", "How?", or "Can you elaborate on that?" to dig deeper.
2. Practice active listening: Pay attention to responses that warrant further exploration.
3. Be flexible with your question order: Be willing to deviate from your planned sequence to pursue important threads.
4. Use the funnel technique: Start with broad questions and narrow down based on responses.

Case Study: Political Interview

During a televised interview in later part of last Indian government, with a politician was asked about a new economic policy, the interviewer asked, "How will this policy affect small & medium businesses?" The politician gave a vague answer about "supporting growth and innovation." Instead of following up to get specifics, the interviewer moved on to the next prepared question about a different topic.

This failure to follow up left viewers without concrete information about the policy's actual impact on small businesses. If the interviewer had asked follow-up questions like, "Can you provide specific examples of how small businesses will be supported?" or "What measurable outcomes do you expect to see for small businesses in the first year of this policy?", they could have elicited more meaningful and informative responses.

In this case, may be the politician also wanted this to be diverted but it was the mistake from interviewer that the lead was missed due to lack of a follow up question.

Asking Insensitive or Inappropriate Questions

Asking questions that cross personal, cultural, or professional boundaries can damage rapport, create discomfort, and potentially lead to ethical or legal issues.

The Problem:

Insensitive or inappropriate questions:

- Can offend or alienate respondents
- May violate ethical guidelines or legal regulations
- Can damage professional relationships or reputations
- May lead to biased or unreliable responses due to respondent discomfort

Examples:

Inappropriate: "How old are you?" (in a job interview context)

Better: "How many years of experience do you have in this field?"

Consequences:

- Damaged rapport or trust with respondents
- Potential legal or ethical violations
- Biased or unreliable data due to respondent discomfort
- Negative impact on the reputation of the researcher or organization

Strategies to Avoid This Pitfall:

1. Be aware of cultural sensitivities: Research cultural norms and taboos, especially when working across cultures.
2. Focus on relevant information: Ensure questions are directly related to the topic at hand.
3. Use inclusive language: Avoid assumptions about gender, race, religion, or other personal characteristics.
4. Provide options to decline: Allow respondents to opt-out of answering sensitive questions.

Case Study: Employment Form

I appeared for an interview during early stage of my career & they gave me a form to fill. I was appearing for a role of sales engineer, but the format was common across jobs & it had questions related to my exposure to manufacturing excellence, ISO audits and even about my key personal information like passport number, health details etc. I felt uncomfortable and violated and not to even pursue that opportunity.

By redesigning the form to include only questions relevant to the specific role and by offering clear explanations for why certain information might be needed (when applicable), the organization could have maintained trust and interest of potential employees and still got the required data points.

In conclusion, effective questioning is a nuanced skill that requires practice, self-awareness, and a genuine commitment to understanding others. By recognizing and avoiding these common pitfalls, we can significantly improve the quality of information we gather, the insights we gain, and the relationships we build through our interactions.

Mastering the art of questioning is a critical skill that can significantly enhance the quality and depth of information gathered in various professional and personal contexts. To improve your questioning techniques, it's essential to start with thorough preparation. This involves not only researching the topic at hand but also familiarizing yourself with the background and expertise of your respondents. Such preparation allows you to craft informed, relevant questions that demonstrate respect for the respondent's time and knowledge while also probing for genuinely insightful information.

Clarity and specificity in questioning are paramount. Ambiguous or vague questions can lead to confusion, misinterpretation, and ultimately, less valuable responses. By formulating clear, precise questions, you guide the respondent towards providing the specific information you seek. This precision not only improves the quality of the data collected but also makes the conversation more efficient and focused.

Active listening is another crucial component of effective questioning. It involves fully concentrating on what is being said rather than passively hearing the words. By paying close attention to responses, you can identify opportunities for follow-up questions that delve deeper into interesting or unexpected points. This skill allows for a more dynamic and productive exchange, often uncovering insights that might have been missed with a more rigid questioning approach.

Maintaining neutrality in your questioning is vital to avoid biasing the responses. Leading questions or those that betray the questioner's own opinions can skew the information gathered, potentially compromising its validity and usefulness. By framing questions in a neutral manner, you encourage honest, unbiased responses that more accurately reflect the respondent's true thoughts and experiences.

Sensitivity and respect for cultural, personal, and professional boundaries are essential in questioning. This involves being aware of potentially sensitive topics and approaching them with tact and consideration. It also means recognizing and respecting the limits of what a respondent may be willing or able to share. By demonstrating this awareness and respect, you create a more comfortable environment for open and honest communication.

Flexibility in questioning is a valuable skill that allows you to adapt to the flow of the conversation. While having a prepared set of questions is important, being willing to deviate from this script when valuable new information emerges can lead to richer, more insightful discussions. This adaptability shows that you are genuinely engaged with the respondent and interested in exploring the most relevant and important aspects of the topic at hand.

Finally, continuous reflection and improvement of your questioning techniques are crucial for long-term success. Regularly reviewing your approach, seeking feedback from others, and analyzing the effectiveness of your questions can help you refine your skills over time. This might involve assessing which types of questions tend to elicit the most valuable responses, identifying areas where you consistently struggle, and actively working to address these challenges.

By incorporating these key takeaways into your questioning practice, you can significantly enhance your ability to gather meaningful information, foster productive dialogues, and gain deeper insights across a wide range of situations. Whether in professional interviews, academic research, or personal conversations, these skills will enable you to navigate complex topics more effectively and build stronger, more insightful connections with others.

By mastering the art of questioning, we open doors to deeper understanding, more meaningful connections, and more effective problem-solving across all areas of professional and personal life. Whether in research, journalism, business, education, or everyday conversations, the ability to ask the right questions in the right way is a powerful tool for unlocking knowledge and fostering productive dialogue.

Cultural Perspectives on Questioning

Cultural perspectives on questioning play a significant role in shaping communication patterns and information-gathering processes across different societies. The approach to questioning can vary dramatically from one culture to another, reflecting deeply ingrained values, social hierarchies, and traditional modes of knowledge transmission. In some cultures, particularly those influenced by Confucian thought in many parts of Asia, direct questioning of authority figures or elders is often viewed as a sign of disrespect or challenge to established wisdom. Students in these contexts may be expected to learn through attentive listening and observation rather than through active questioning, which can be seen as disrupting the harmony of the learning environment. This stands in stark contrast to the Western Socratic tradition, which not only encourages but often celebrates vigorous questioning as a fundamental tool for critical thinking and the pursuit of knowledge.

The nuances of cultural questioning styles extend beyond the simple dichotomy of direct versus indirect approaches. For instance, in many Native American cultures, a more circuitous path to information-gathering is often preferred. Rather than posing direct questions, individuals might share related stories or observations, creating a context that invites others to contribute relevant information or insights. This indirect method of questioning aligns with cultural values that prioritize communal knowledge-sharing and respect for individual experiences. Similarly, in some Middle Eastern cultures, the art of questioning may involve a dance of hospitality and relationship-building before delving into the core inquiry, reflecting the importance placed on personal connections in these societies.

Understanding and navigating these cultural differences in questioning styles has become increasingly crucial in our globalized world. As international collaborations, multicultural workplaces, and cross-border communications become more common, the ability to adapt one's questioning approach to different cultural contexts can significantly enhance the effectiveness of information exchange and relationship-building. Misunderstandings arising from culturally insensitive questioning can lead to communication breakdowns, missed opportunities, or even offense. Conversely, demonstrating awareness and respect for diverse questioning norms can foster trust, facilitate more open and productive dialogues, and lead to richer, more nuanced understandings across cultural boundaries. This cultural competence in questioning is not just about avoiding faux pas; it's about creating bridges of understanding that can lead to more innovative, inclusive, and effective global interactions in fields ranging from business and diplomacy to education and scientific research.

The Art of Questioning in Today's digital world:

As we delve deeper into the digital era, the landscape of questioning is undergoing a profound transformation, reshaping how we seek and process information. The advent of powerful search engines has revolutionized our approach to factual inquiries, providing instant access to vast repositories of knowledge at our fingertips. This shift has fundamentally altered the nature of human questioning, steering us towards more complex, nuanced, and interpretative inquiries that extend beyond mere fact-finding. The ease with which we can now obtain basic information has elevated the importance of asking deeper, more insightful questions that challenge our understanding and push the boundaries of knowledge.

Artificial Intelligence (AI) and machine learning technologies are at the forefront of this evolution, dramatically reshaping the questioning landscape. Advanced AI systems, exemplified by virtual assistants like Siri, Alexa, and Google Assistant, have made significant strides in comprehending and responding to natural language questions. These systems are continuously improving their ability to interpret context, nuance, and even emotion in human queries, offering increasingly sophisticated and personalized responses. This progress in AI-driven question-answering capabilities is not only changing how we interact with technology but also raising important questions about the future role of human inquiry in an age where machines can provide quick, accurate answers to a wide range of questions.

However, this technological advancement brings with it a set of critical challenges and considerations. As we become more reliant on AI and automated systems for answers, there is a growing concern about the potential erosion of human questioning skills. The ability to formulate incisive, probing questions is a fundamental aspect of critical thinking and problem-solving. There is a risk that over-dependence on AI for answers could lead to a diminishment of these crucial cognitive skills. This raises important questions about how we can maintain and cultivate the art of asking good questions in an environment where instant answers are readily available. Educators, in particular, face the challenge of developing curricula and teaching methods that emphasize the importance of questioning skills, critical thinking, and analytical reasoning in a world where factual information is easily accessible.

The digital age has also ushered in an era of information overload and the proliferation of misinformation, colloquially known as "fake news." This phenomenon underscores the growing importance of developing sophisticated questioning skills to navigate the complex information landscape. In an environment where anyone can publish and disseminate information widely, the ability to ask probing questions, verify sources, and think critically about the content we consume has become more crucial than ever. This situation highlights the need for digital literacy skills that go beyond mere technological proficiency, encompassing the ability to evaluate information critically, understand biases, and discern credible sources from unreliable ones.

Looking ahead, the future of questioning in the digital age is likely to involve a delicate balance between leveraging technological advancements and preserving human cognitive skills. We may see the emergence of new questioning techniques and methodologies designed specifically for the digital era, combining the strengths of human intuition and creativity with the processing power and data analysis capabilities of AI. There could be a greater emphasis on teaching metacognitive skills – learning how to learn and how to ask questions effectively in a world of abundant information.

Moreover, the evolution of questioning in the digital age may lead to new forms of collaborative inquiry, where humans and AI systems work together to explore complex problems and generate innovative solutions. This symbiotic relationship could potentially enhance our ability to ask more profound questions and tackle increasingly complex challenges across various fields of study and professional domains.

In conclusion, the future of questioning in the digital age presents both exciting opportunities and significant challenges. As we navigate this evolving landscape, it will be crucial to harness the power of technology while simultaneously nurturing and refining our human capacity for inquiry, critical thinking, and creative problem-solving. The ability to ask the right questions – to probe deeply, think critically, and challenge assumptions – will remain a vital skill, perhaps even more so in an age where answers are abundant but wisdom and discernment are increasingly precious commodities.

Practical Tips and Exercises to Improve Questioning Skills:

In our quest for knowledge and understanding, the ability to ask effective questions is paramount. Questions are the keys that unlock doors to new insights, drive innovation, and foster deeper connections with others. This section of the book will delve into practical exercises designed to enhance your questioning skills, enabling you to become a more adept communicator, problem-solver, and critical thinker.

The Foundations of Effective Questioning

Before we dive into the exercises, it's crucial to understand the fundamental principles that underpin effective questioning:

The Anatomy of a Good Question

A good question is:

- Clear and concise
- Open-ended when appropriate
- Relevant to the context
- Thought-provoking
- Free from bias or assumption

The Impact of Questioning in Various Fields

Effective questioning plays a vital role in:

- Scientific inquiry
- Journalistic investigation
- Business strategy
- Educational pedagogy
- Personal growth and self-reflection

The Psychology Behind Questioning

Understanding the cognitive processes involved in formulating and processing questions can help us ask better ones. This subsection would explore:

- The role of curiosity in questioning
- How questions affect memory and learning
- The impact of questions on social interactions

Exercise 1: The Five Whys Technique

Origin and Purpose

The Five Whys technique, originally developed by Sakichi Toyoda for the Toyota Motor Corporation, is a simple yet powerful tool for uncovering the root cause of a problem or situation.

How to Practice the Five Whys

1. Identify a problem or situation you want to explore.
2. Ask "Why?" in response to the problem.
3. Take the answer to your first "Why?" and ask "Why?" again.
4. Repeat this process at least five times.

Example of the Five Whys in Action

Problem: "Sales are declining."

1. Why are sales declining?

- Because customers are buying less.

2. Why are customers buying less?

- Because they don't see the value in our product.

3. Why don't they see the value in our product?

- Because we haven't effectively communicated its benefits.

4. Why haven't we effectively communicated its benefits?

- Because our marketing strategy is outdated.

5. Why is our marketing strategy outdated?

- Because we haven't invested in market research and new marketing channels.

Benefits of the Five Whys Technique

- Encourages deeper analysis
- Helps identify root causes rather than symptoms
- Promotes systemic thinking

Variations and Advanced Applications

- The "Five Hows" for solution-focused thinking
- Combining the Five Whys with other problem-solving tools

Exercises for Mastering the Five Whys

1. Personal Problem Solving: Apply the Five Whys to a personal challenge you're facing.
2. Organizational Analysis: Use the technique to explore a business or organizational issue.
3. Historical Events: Practice applying the Five Whys to historical events to uncover underlying causes.

Exercise 2: Question Reframing

The Power of Perspective

Reframing questions allows us to approach problems from different angles, often leading to innovative solutions and deeper understanding.

Techniques for Question Reframing

1. Change the scope (broader or narrower)
2. Alter the timeframe (past, present, future)
3. Shift the perspective (different stakeholders)
4. Modify the assumption
5. Transform negative questions into positive ones

Example of Question Reframing

Original question: "How can we increase sales?"

Reframed versions:

1. "What factors are currently limiting our sales growth?"
2. "How might our sales strategy evolve over the next five years?"
3. "From our customers' perspective, what would make our product more appealing?"

4. "What if we focused on customer retention instead of new acquisitions?"

5. "How can we create more value for our existing customers?"

Benefits of Question Reframing

- Breaks mental blocks
- Encourages creative thinking
- Reveals hidden assumptions
- Provides a more comprehensive understanding of the issue

Exercises for Mastering Question Reframing

1. Daily Reframing Challenge: Take a common question you encounter each day and reframe it in five different ways.

2. Problem-Solving Workshop: In a group, practice reframing a complex problem from multiple perspectives.

3. Media Headline Reframing: Take news headlines and reframe them to reveal potential biases or alternative viewpoints.

Exercise 3: Active Listening for Better Questioning

The Connection Between Listening and Questioning

Active listening is a crucial skill that complements and enhances our ability to ask effective questions.

Principles of Active Listening

- Give full attention to the speaker
- Avoid interrupting
- Use non-verbal cues to show engagement
- Paraphrase to ensure understanding
- Suspend judgment

Techniques for Integrating Active Listening and Questioning

1. Reflective Questioning: Formulate questions based on what you've heard to clarify and deepen understanding.

2. Empathetic Inquiry: Ask questions that demonstrate you've understood the speaker's emotions and perspective.

3. Contextual Probing: Use the information provided to ask more informed, relevant follow-up questions.

Example of Active Listening Leading to Effective Questioning

Scenario: A colleague is discussing a project challenge.

Colleague: "We're behind schedule on the project because the client keeps changing their requirements."

Poor response: "Why didn't you anticipate these changes?"

Active listening response: "It sounds like the changing requirements are causing significant delays. Can you tell me more about the nature of these changes? How do you think we could better manage client expectations in the future?"

Benefits of Combining Active Listening with Questioning

- Builds rapport and trust
- Leads to more insightful and relevant questions
- Improves overall communication effectiveness

Exercises for Developing Active Listening Skills

1. The Silent Minute: Practice listening to someone for one full minute without interrupting, then formulate three questions based on what you heard.
2. Paraphrase and Question: In conversations, make a habit of paraphrasing what you've heard before asking your next question.
3. Emotion Recognition: Practice identifying the emotions behind what someone is saying and ask questions that address these underlying feelings.

Exercise 4: The Question Journal

The Value of Reflection in Skill Development

Keeping a question journal allows you to track your progress, identify patterns in your questioning, and continuously improve your skills.

How to Maintain a Question Journal

1. Record interesting questions you encounter or create
2. Note the context in which the question arose
3. Reflect on what makes the question effective or ineffective
4. Consider how the question could be improved or expanded

Example Question Journal Entry

Date: October 5, 2023

Question: "What would our business look like if we had to start over from scratch today?"

Context: Brainstorming session for company strategy

Effectiveness: This question is powerful because it challenges assumptions and encourages innovative thinking. It forces us to consider current market conditions and technological advancements that might not have been present when the company was founded.

Potential improvements: Could be made more specific by focusing on particular aspects of the business, e.g., "If we were starting our product development from scratch today, what technologies would we prioritize?"

Benefits of Keeping a Question Journal

- Increases awareness of questioning habits
- Provides a resource for future brainstorming
- Encourages continuous improvement in questioning skills

Exercises for Maximizing Your Question Journal

1. Daily Question Challenge: Commit to adding at least one new question to your journal every day.

2. Question Analysis: Regularly review your journal and categorize questions based on their effectiveness, context, or type.

3. Collaborative Journaling: Share and discuss entries with a peer or mentor to gain new perspectives on your questioning skills.

Exercise 5: Socratic Dialogue Practice

Understanding the Socratic Method

The Socratic method, named after the ancient Greek philosopher Socrates, is a form of cooperative argumentative dialogue between individuals based on asking and answering questions to stimulate critical thinking and draw out ideas and underlying presuppositions.

Principles of Socratic Questioning

- Ask open-ended questions
- Probe assumptions
- Seek evidence
- Explore implications and consequences
- Question the question

Conducting a Socratic Dialogue

1. Choose a topic or concept to explore
2. Begin with a general question about the topic
3. Listen carefully to the response
4. Ask follow-up questions that challenge assumptions or seek clarification
5. Continue the process, gradually refining the discussion and deepening understanding

Example of a Socratic Dialogue

Topic: The nature of justice

Questioner: "What is justice?"

Respondent: "Justice is treating everyone equally under the law."

Questioner: "Is treating everyone equally always just?"

Respondent: "Well, I suppose there might be exceptions..."

Questioner: "Can you think of an example where treating people unequally might be more just?"

Respondent: "Perhaps in cases where some individuals have disadvantages that others don't..."

Questioner: "So, does this mean that justice sometimes requires considering individual circumstances?"

Benefits of Practicing Socratic Dialogue

- Enhances critical thinking skills
- Improves ability to construct logical arguments
- Develops deeper understanding of complex topics
- Strengthens ability to ask probing, thought-provoking questions

Exercises for Mastering Socratic Dialogue

1. One-on-One Practice: Engage in a Socratic dialogue with a partner on a chosen topic for 15 minutes, taking turns as the questioner.
2. Group Socratic Seminar: Facilitate a group discussion using Socratic questioning techniques.
3. Self-Socratic Journaling: Apply Socratic questioning to your own beliefs and ideas in a written format.

Exercise 6: Media Analysis for Question Identification

The Role of Questions in Media and Journalism

Understanding the questions that drive news stories and media content can enhance our critical thinking and media literacy skills.

Techniques for Analyzing Media Through a Questioning Lens

1. Identify the central question(s) the piece is addressing
2. Consider what questions are left unanswered
3. Examine the assumptions underlying the questions being asked
4. Evaluate the effectiveness of how questions are framed and answered

Example Media Analysis

Article Headline: "New Study Shows Correlation Between Social Media Use and Depression in Teens"

Central Questions:

1. How does social media use affect teen mental health?
2. What specific aspects of social media contribute to depression?

Unanswered Questions:

1. Are there any positive effects of social media on teen mental health?
2. How do these findings compare to previous studies on the topic?
3. What recommendations do the researchers make based on their findings?

Assumptions:

1. The correlation implies causation

2. All forms of social media have similar effects

3. The study's methodology is sound and representative

Benefits of Media Analysis for Questioning Skills

- Enhances critical thinking and media literacy
- Improves ability to identify gaps in information
- Develops skill in recognizing underlying assumptions and biases

Exercises for Developing Media Analysis Skills

1. Daily News Question Challenge: Choose a news article each day and identify the key questions it addresses and those it overlooks.

2. Comparative Media Analysis: Compare how different news sources frame questions about the same event or issue.

3. Create Alternative Headlines: Practice rewriting headlines as questions to reveal potential biases or alternative perspectives.

Exercise 7: Reverse Engineering Questions from Solutions

The Value of Working Backwards

Reverse engineering questions from existing solutions can help develop a more solution-oriented mindset and improve problem-solving skills.

Steps for Reverse Engineering Questions

1. Identify a solution or innovation
2. Consider what problem this solution addresses
3. Formulate the question that might have led to this solution
4. Explore alternative questions that could have resulted in similar solutions

Example of Reverse Engineering Questions

Solution: The development of noise-cancelling headphones

Possible questions that led to this innovation:

1. "How can we reduce unwanted ambient noise for headphone users?"
2. "Is it possible to create a personal quiet space in noisy environments?"
3. "Can we use sound waves to counteract other sound waves?"

Benefits of Reverse Engineering Questions

- Enhances problem-solving skills
- Encourages innovative thinking
- Improves ability to identify root issues and needs

Exercises for Practicing Reverse Engineering

1. Innovation Analysis: Choose a recent technological innovation and try to reverse engineer the questions that led to its development.

2. Historical Breakthroughs: Apply this technique to significant historical inventions or discoveries.

3. Personal Problem-Solving: Reflect on a recent personal solution you've implemented and reverse engineer the question that prompted it.

Exercise 8: Cultural Question Swap

The Importance of Cultural Sensitivity in Questioning

In our increasingly globalized world, the ability to adapt our questioning style to different cultural contexts is crucial for effective communication and understanding.

Techniques for Culturally Adaptive Questioning

1. Research cultural norms and communication styles
2. Consider indirect vs. direct questioning approaches
3. Be aware of potentially sensitive topics
4. Adapt question structure and formality as appropriate

Example of Cultural Question Adaptation

Western context: "What do you think about this proposal?"

Adapted for some Asian contexts: "I would be honored to hear your thoughts on this proposal."

Benefits of Practicing Cultural Question Adaptation

- Improves cross-cultural communication skills
- Enhances cultural sensitivity and awareness
- Reduces the risk of misunderstandings or offense

Exercises for Developing Cultural Question Adaptation Skills

1. Cultural Research and Reframing: Choose a culture different from your own, research its communication norms, and practice reframing common questions to suit that culture.

2. Role-Playing Scenarios: Engage in role-playing exercises where you must adapt your questioning style to different cultural contexts.

3. International News Analysis: Examine how questions are framed in international news sources and consider how they might be adapted for different cultural audiences.

As we conclude this comprehensive exploration of practical exercises to improve questioning skills, it's important to remember that becoming a skilled questioner is an ongoing journey. By consistently applying these exercises and techniques in various aspects of your life, you can dramatically enhance your ability to gather information, solve problems, and connect with others.

Key Takeaways

- Effective questioning is a skill that can be developed through deliberate practice

- Different questioning techniques are suited to different situations and objectives
- Cultural sensitivity and active listening are crucial components of effective questioning
- Regular reflection and analysis of your questioning habits can lead to continuous improvement

As you continue to hone your questioning skills, remember that the goal is not just to ask more questions, but to ask better ones. Questions have the power to change perspectives, drive innovation, and deepen understanding. By mastering the art of questioning, you equip yourself with a powerful tool for personal growth, professional success, and meaningful engagement with the world around you.

Embracing the Question-Driven Life

As we've explored throughout this chapter, the art of asking the right questions is a powerful tool for navigating the complexities of our world. From scientific discovery to personal growth, from business innovation to social change, the right questions can unlock new possibilities and lead us to more meaningful answers. The exercises we've discussed, such as the Five Whys technique, question reframing, and Socratic dialogue, provide practical methods for developing this crucial skill. By applying these techniques in various contexts, we can train our minds to approach problems and situations from multiple angles, uncovering insights that might otherwise remain hidden.

By honing our questioning skills, we can become more effective problem-solvers, more engaged learners, and more insightful thinkers. We can challenge assumptions, uncover hidden truths, and push the boundaries of human knowledge. The practice of keeping a question journal, for instance, allows us to reflect on our questioning habits and continuously refine our approach. Similarly, the exercise of reverse engineering questions from solutions encourages us to think critically about the origins of innovations and breakthroughs, fostering a more creative and solution-oriented mindset.

In a world of rapid change and information overload, the ability to ask good questions is more valuable than ever. It allows us to cut through the noise, focus on what's truly important, and continue growing and adapting throughout our lives. The media analysis exercise we discussed is particularly relevant in this context, as it helps us navigate the complex landscape of modern information by identifying the key questions driving news stories and recognizing those left unasked.

As the philosopher Claude Levi-Strauss once said, "The scientist is not a person who gives the right answers, he's one who asks the right questions." This wisdom extends beyond science to all areas of life. By embracing a question-driven approach to life, we open ourselves to continuous learning, growth, and discovery. The cultural question swap exercise underscores the importance of this approach in our increasingly globalized world, reminding us that effective questioning must be adaptable to different cultural contexts and perspectives.

So let us cultivate our curiosity, refine our questioning skills, and never stop asking: What if? Why? How? These simple words, when used thoughtfully and persistently, have the power to transform our understanding of ourselves and the world around us. The active listening exercise we explored demonstrates how these questions can be even more powerful when combined with genuine attentiveness to others, leading to deeper connections and more meaningful dialogues.

In the end, it's not just about finding the right answers, but about asking the right questions. For in the asking lies the seed of all human progress and understanding. As we continue to practice and refine our questioning skills using the exercises outlined in this chapter, we equip ourselves with a versatile and powerful tool for personal growth, professional success, and meaningful engagement with the complex world around us. The journey of becoming a skilled questioner is ongoing, but with consistent practice and reflection, we can unlock new levels of insight and understanding in every aspect of our lives.

CHAPTER FOUR

The Nature of Answers

In our quest for knowledge and understanding, we constantly seek answers to questions that range from the mundane to the profound. But what exactly constitutes an answer? How do we distinguish between a true answer and something that merely resembles one? This chapter delves deep into the nature of answers, exploring their characteristics, types, and the various factors that determine their validity and usefulness.

What is an answer:

At its core, an answer is a response to a question or inquiry. It's an attempt to provide information, clarification, or resolution to a particular query or problem. However, this simple definition belies the complexity inherent in the concept of an answer.

Characteristics of a Valid Answer:

A valid answer is a cornerstone of effective communication and problem-solving, embodying a set of essential qualities that ensure its reliability and usefulness. At its core, a valid answer must be **relevant**, directly addressing the question or problem at hand without straying into tangential or unrelated topics. This relevance ensures that the answer provides meaningful insight and contributes to the resolution of the issue being discussed. It demonstrates a clear understanding of the query and a focused approach to addressing it.

Accuracy is another crucial aspect of a valid answer. It must provide correct and factual information, free from errors or misrepresentations. This requires a thorough understanding of the subject matter and a commitment to truthfulness. In academic or professional contexts, this often involves citing reputable sources and cross-referencing information to ensure its veracity. Inaccurate information, even if well-intentioned, can lead to misunderstandings, poor decision-making, and potentially harmful consequences.

Completeness is equally important in crafting a valid answer. A truly comprehensive response covers all aspects of the question, leaving no significant gaps in the explanation or analysis. This often requires considering multiple perspectives and addressing potential counterarguments or exceptions. A complete answer anticipates follow-up questions and provides a well-rounded view of the topic, demonstrating a deep understanding of its complexities and nuances.

Clarity is a key characteristic that ensures the answer's effectiveness in conveying information. A valid answer must be expressed in a clear and understandable manner, using language appropriate for the intended audience. This involves organizing thoughts logically, avoiding jargon or overly technical language when unnecessary, and presenting ideas in a coherent structure. Clarity in communication helps prevent misinterpretations and ensures that the answer's value is fully realized by those receiving it.

Verifiability adds a layer of credibility to a valid answer. It means that the information provided can be tested or confirmed through observation, experimentation, or reference to authoritative sources. This quality is particularly important in scientific and academic contexts, where peer review and replication of results are standard practices. Even in everyday situations, the ability to back up an answer with evidence or logical reasoning enhances its validity and persuasiveness.

These characteristics of a valid answer - relevance, accuracy, completeness, clarity, and verifiability - are interconnected and mutually reinforcing. An answer that excels in all these areas is not only intellectually sound but also practically useful. It provides a solid foundation for further discussion, decision-making, or action. In educational settings, answers that embody these qualities demonstrate a student's mastery of the subject matter and critical thinking skills. In professional environments, they contribute to effective problem-solving and informed decision-making.

It's worth noting that the relative importance of these characteristics may vary depending on the context. For instance, in a brainstorming session, the emphasis might be more on relevance and completeness, encouraging a wide range of ideas, while in a scientific paper, accuracy and verifiability would take precedence. Understanding the balance of these qualities in different situations is a skill in itself, one that develops with experience and practice.

In short, a valid answer is more than just a correct response; it's a carefully crafted piece of communication that addresses the question comprehensively, accurately, and clearly, while also being relevant and verifiable. By striving to incorporate these qualities in our answers, we enhance the quality of our discourse, improve our problem-solving capabilities, and contribute more effectively to knowledge and understanding in both personal and professional spheres. It's important to note that the validity of an answer can sometimes be subjective, depending on the context, the person asking the question, and the field of inquiry. What constitutes a satisfactory answer in one context may not suffice in another.

Different type of Answers

Factual Answers provide concrete, verifiable information in response to straightforward questions. These answers are rooted in objective data and are typically used when dealing with quantifiable or easily observable facts. In the sales and marketing domain, a factual answer might address a query about a company's market share or product specifications. For example, if asked about the revenue of a major tech company, a factual answer would provide the exact figure from the most recent financial report, such as "Apple's total net sales for the fiscal year 2023 were $383.29 billion." This type of answer leaves little room for interpretation and is based on publicly available, reliable data.

Analytical Answers involve a deeper level of interpretation and often connect various pieces of information to provide insights. These answers go beyond simply stating facts and require critical thinking to draw meaningful conclusions. In sales and marketing, analytical answers are crucial for understanding market trends, consumer behavior, or campaign performance. For instance, when analyzing the effectiveness of a multi-channel marketing campaign, an analytical answer might examine the conversion rates across different platforms, compare them to industry benchmarks, and provide insights on which channels performed best and why. This type of answer might conclude, "The email marketing channel outperformed social media advertising by 25% in terms of conversion rate, likely due to the more personalized nature of email communications and the ability to segment the audience more effectively."

Theoretical Answers are based on established theories or hypotheses and often deal with abstract concepts that can't be directly observed. In sales and marketing, theoretical answers are particularly useful when discussing consumer psychology, brand positioning, or marketing strategies. These answers often draw from academic research and established models in the field. For example, when explaining the concept of brand equity, a theoretical answer might reference Keller's Customer-Based Brand Equity model, explaining how brand awareness, brand associations, perceived quality, and brand loyalty contribute to overall brand equity. The answer might illustrate this with a hypothetical scenario: "Consider a luxury car brand like Mercedes-Benz. Its strong brand equity is built on high brand awareness, positive associations with luxury and performance, perceived high quality, and a loyal customer base. This theoretical framework helps explain why Mercedes-Benz can command premium prices and maintain market share even in competitive markets."

Opinion-Based Answers reflect personal views or judgments and, while they may be informed by facts, are inherently subjective. In sales and marketing, opinion-based answers are often sought when dealing with creative decisions, strategy formulation, or predictions about future trends. These answers draw on the respondent's experience and expertise to provide valuable insights. For instance, if asked about the future of influencer marketing, an opinion-based answer might state, "In my view, micro-influencers will become increasingly important in the next five years. While celebrity endorsements have been the norm, I believe that consumers are growing more skeptical of large-scale influencers and are seeking more authentic, niche-specific recommendations. Companies that pivot towards partnering with smaller, highly engaged influencers in specific niches are likely to see better engagement rates and return on investment."

Procedural Answers provide step-by-step instructions or explanations of how to accomplish a specific task. In sales and marketing, these answers are crucial for implementing strategies, using tools, or following best practices. Procedural answers break down complex processes into manageable steps, making them easier to understand and execute. For example, a procedural answer explaining how to create a customer persona might outline the following steps:

1. Gather data from multiple sources including customer surveys, sales data, and website analytics.

2. Identify patterns and commonalities in the data to segment your audience.

3. Create a detailed profile for each segment, including demographics, behaviors, goals, and pain points.

4. Give each persona a name and a stock photo to make them more relatable.

5. Validate your personas with your sales and customer service teams.

6. Use these personas to inform your marketing strategies and product development.

This type of answer provides a clear roadmap for marketers to follow when developing customer personas, a crucial element in targeted marketing strategies.

The Structure of Answers

Direct Answers are characterized by their immediate and straightforward approach to addressing a question. These responses cut to the heart of the matter, providing the requested information without unnecessary elaboration or context. Direct answers are particularly valuable when clarity and efficiency are paramount, such as in time-sensitive situations or when dealing with factual queries. In a business setting, direct answers are often preferred in high-level meetings or when communicating with executives who need quick, actionable information. For example, if a sales manager asks, "What was our total revenue for Q3?" a direct answer would be, "Our total revenue for Q3 was $2.5 million." This type of answer leaves no room for ambiguity and allows for immediate understanding and decision-making based on the provided information.

Indirect Answers take a more nuanced approach by providing context or additional information before addressing the main question. This structure is particularly useful when the answer requires background knowledge or when the question is complex and multifaceted. Indirect answers can help frame the response in a way that enhances understanding and provides a more comprehensive view of the subject matter. In marketing strategy discussions, for instance, an indirect answer might be appropriate when addressing a question about entering a new market. The response might begin by outlining current market trends, discussing potential challenges, and then finally recommending a course of action. This approach ensures that the answer is not only informative but also well-reasoned and contextualized within the broader business landscape.

Partial Answers address only a portion of a question or provide incomplete information. While not ideal, partial answers can be valuable in situations where complete information is not available or when addressing complex queries with multiple components. In the realm of market research, a partial answer might occur when responding to a question about consumer preferences across different demographics. The answer might provide detailed insights into certain age groups or geographic regions while acknowledging that data for other segments is still being collected or analyzed. Partial answers can serve as a starting point for further investigation or discussion, highlighting areas where additional research or information gathering is needed.

Null Answers indicate that no information is available or that the question cannot be answered with the current knowledge or resources at hand. While it might seem counterintuitive, null answers can be extremely valuable in business settings as they prevent the spread of misinformation and highlight areas where further research or data collection is necessary. For example, if asked about the performance of a new product in a specific market where it hasn't been launched yet, a null answer would be appropriate: "We currently don't have any data on the product's performance in that market as it hasn't been introduced there yet." This type of answer demonstrates honesty and accuracy, which are crucial in maintaining credibility and trust in professional relationships. Furthermore, null answers can serve as catalysts for initiating new research projects, market studies, or data collection efforts to fill the identified knowledge gaps.

The importance of Context in Answers

The importance of context in answers cannot be overstated, particularly in the realm of sales and marketing. This multifaceted concept encompasses various dimensions that profoundly impact the effectiveness and relevance of responses in professional settings.

Cultural context plays a pivotal role in shaping both questions and answers within the sales and marketing domain. For instance, a marketing campaign that resonates well with consumers in the United States might fall flat or even offend audiences in Japan due to differing cultural norms and values. A prime example is the Procter & Gamble's Febreze air freshener launch in Japan, which initially failed because the product's strong scents were off-putting to Japanese consumers who prefer subtler fragrances.

Understanding and respecting these cultural nuances is crucial for crafting appropriate and effective marketing messages.

Historical context is equally significant, as it reflects the evolving nature of consumer preferences and market trends. What was once considered a groundbreaking marketing strategy may become obsolete or even counterproductive over time. The tobacco industry serves as a stark example of this shift. In the mid-20th century, cigarette advertisements were commonplace and even featured endorsements from medical professionals. However, as public awareness of the health risks associated with smoking grew, such marketing tactics became not only ineffective but also highly controversial and ultimately banned in many countries.

The **disciplinary context** in sales and marketing is particularly crucial, as it defines the standards and best practices within the field. Different industries and market segments may require distinct approaches to sales and marketing. For example, the business-to-business (B2B) sales process often involves longer decision-making cycles and multiple stakeholders, necessitating a more relationship-focused approach. In contrast, business-to-consumer (B2C) marketing might emphasize emotional appeals and instant gratification. A software company selling enterprise solutions would employ vastly different marketing strategies compared to a fast-food chain targeting individual consumers.

Personal context, encompassing an individual's knowledge, experiences, and beliefs, significantly influences how marketing messages are perceived and interpreted. This is why personalization has become a cornerstone of modern marketing strategies. For instance, Amazon's product recommendations based on a user's browsing and purchase history exemplify how personal context can be leveraged to enhance marketing effectiveness. Similarly, sales professionals often tailor their pitches to address the specific pain points and preferences of individual clients, recognizing that a one-size-fits-all approach is rarely successful in today's diverse marketplace.

In conclusion, the importance of context in answers within the sales and marketing domain cannot be overstated. Cultural, historical, disciplinary, and personal contexts all play crucial roles in shaping effective communication strategies. By carefully considering these contextual factors, sales and marketing professionals can craft more relevant, impactful, and successful campaigns and interactions with their target audiences.

Answering is a Process & not an Art:

The process of answering a question is a multifaceted endeavor that requires careful consideration and a systematic approach. It begins with a crucial step: understanding the question at hand. This involves carefully parsing the query, identifying key terms, and discerning the underlying intent of the person asking. For example, if someone asks, "What are the long-term effects of climate change?", it's essential to recognize that they're not just looking for a list of effects, but rather a comprehensive analysis of how these changes might unfold over time.

Once the question is fully comprehended, the next phase is gathering information. This step is akin to detective work, where one must diligently collect relevant data from various sources. This could involve conducting extensive research using academic databases, consulting expert opinions, or even performing experiments to obtain firsthand data. For instance, to answer a question about the impact of social media on mental health, one might review recent psychological studies, analyze user behavior data, and perhaps even conduct surveys to gather fresh insights.

With a wealth of information at hand, the process moves into the critical stage of analysis and synthesis. This is where the collected data is carefully examined, patterns are identified, and connections are drawn. It's not merely about regurgitating facts, but rather about weaving together disparate pieces of information into a coherent narrative. For example, when addressing a question about the future of renewable energy, one would need to analyze trends in technology development, policy changes, and market dynamics to paint a comprehensive picture of potential scenarios.

The final step in the process is formulating the answer. This is where all the previous work culminates in a clear, concise, and appropriate response. The formulation should be tailored to the context and the intended audience. For a technical question about quantum computing, the answer might include complex mathematical equations and technical jargon. In contrast, a response to a question about healthy eating habits for children would be presented in simple, accessible language with practical examples. The key is to articulate the answer in a manner that not only addresses the question accurately but also engages the listener or reader effectively.

Not Every Response is an Answer:

In the realm of question-answering, it's crucial to understand not only what constitutes a valid answer but also what falls short of this standard. A detailed exploration of "what cannot be considered an answer" reveals several categories of responses that fail to meet the criteria for a genuine answer.

Inadequate Responses

Irrelevant Information

One of the most common pitfalls in answering questions is providing information that, while potentially true or interesting, does not address the specific query at hand. For instance, if asked about the economic impact of a particular policy, a response detailing the policy's history without addressing its economic consequences would not be considered an answer. This type of response often occurs when the respondent has limited knowledge of the subject matter or misunderstands the question's intent.

Circular Reasoning

Answers that merely restate the question or use the conclusion as a premise fail to provide new information or insight. A classic example of this is the response "It is what it is" to a question asking for an explanation of a phenomenon. Such responses create a logical loop that offers no substantive information and leaves the questioner no more informed than before.

Logical Fallacies

Responses built on faulty reasoning, regardless of their apparent plausibility, cannot be considered valid answers. For example, an argument from authority (e.g., "It must be true because a famous person said so") does not constitute a legitimate answer, as it relies on the speaker's status rather than factual evidence or logical reasoning.

Problematic Responses

Unsupported Claims

Statements made without evidence or logical reasoning, especially in academic or scientific contexts, fall short of being answers. For instance, if asked about the cause of a particular disease, a response attributing it to supernatural forces without any scientific basis would not be considered a valid answer in a medical context.

Ambiguous or Vague Statements

Responses that are too unclear or open to multiple interpretations often fail to qualify as answers. If asked about the timeline for a project's completion, a response like "in the near future" is too vague to be useful and thus cannot be considered a proper answer. Effective answers should provide specific, actionable information.

Incomplete or Partial Responses

While partial information can be valuable, responses that address only a fraction of the question without acknowledging their incompleteness are problematic. For example, if asked about the factors contributing to climate change, a response that only mentions carbon dioxide emissions without addressing other greenhouse gases or human activities would be incomplete.

Ethical and Philosophical Considerations

Misleading or Deceptive Responses

Answers that intentionally mislead or deceive, even if they contain elements of truth, cannot be considered valid. This includes responses that cherry-pick data to support a predetermined conclusion while ignoring contradictory evidence.

Responses to Unanswerable Questions

Some questions, particularly in philosophy or theoretical physics, may be inherently unanswerable due to logical paradoxes or limitations in human knowledge. In such cases, explaining why the question cannot be answered definitively is more appropriate than attempting to provide a concrete answer.

Ethical Dilemmas

In cases involving complex ethical considerations, a single, definitive answer may not exist. For instance, questions about the morality of certain actions in extreme scenarios often fall into this category. While discussing various perspectives and ethical frameworks can be valuable, presenting a single viewpoint as the definitive answer would be inappropriate.

Understanding what cannot be considered an answer is as crucial as knowing what constitutes a valid one. It encourages critical thinking, promotes intellectual honesty, and fosters more meaningful and productive discussions. By recognizing these pitfalls, we can strive for higher-quality discourse and more effective problem-solving across all domains of knowledge.

CHAPTER FIVE

The Anatomy of Stupidity: Dissecting Flawed Answers

In our quest for knowledge and understanding, we often encounter responses that fall short of providing genuine insight or solutions. These flawed answers, born from various forms of cognitive missteps, form the foundation of what we commonly refer to as stupidity. However, stupidity is not merely a lack of intelligence; it is a complex phenomenon with deep roots in human psychology and behaviour.

The anatomy of stupidity encompasses a wide range of factors, from cognitive biases and logical fallacies to psychological resistance and self-deception. By dissecting these flawed answers, we can gain valuable insights into the human mind's workings and the challenges we face in our pursuit of knowledge and rational thinking.

At its core, stupidity often manifests as a failure to process information effectively or to apply knowledge appropriately. This can result in responses that are irrelevant, circular, or based on faulty reasoning. For instance, when faced with a complex question about climate change, a flawed answer might oversimplify the issue or rely on anecdotal evidence rather than scientific data.

Cognitive biases play a significant role in shaping these flawed responses. Our brains, in an attempt to navigate the overwhelming amount of information we encounter daily, rely on mental shortcuts that can lead us astray. These biases can cause us to cling to preexisting beliefs, even in the face of contradictory evidence, or to make hasty generalizations based on limited information.

Moreover, psychological resistance often underlies our inability to recognize and correct our own flawed thinking. This resistance can stem from a fear of acknowledging our ignorance or a deep-seated belief in our own infallibility. As a result, we may stubbornly adhere to incorrect ideas or reject new information that challenges our worldview.

Understanding the anatomy of stupidity is not merely an academic exercise; it has profound implications for decision-making, problem-solving, and social interactions. By examining flawed answers and the mechanisms behind them, we can develop strategies to overcome our cognitive limitations and foster more rational, effective thinking.

In this exploration, we will delve into the various components that contribute to flawed answers, from the psychological underpinnings to the logical errors that often go unnoticed. By dissecting these elements, we aim to shed light on the nature of stupidity and provide tools for recognizing and combating it in ourselves and others.

What Makes an Answer Stupid?

What makes an answer stupid is a complex interplay of cognitive, psychological, and contextual factors that result in a response that fails to address the question adequately or provide meaningful insight. Stupidity in answers is not merely a reflection of intellectual capacity but often stems from a combination of cognitive biases, logical fallacies, and a fundamental misunderstanding of the subject matter or the question itself.

At its core, a stupid answer often lacks **logical coherence**, failing to connect ideas in a meaningful way or draw valid conclusions from the available information. For instance, if asked about the causes of climate change, a stupid answer might attribute it solely to natural cycles without considering the overwhelming scientific evidence of human influence. This disregard for established facts is another hallmark of stupid answers, where personal beliefs or unfounded opinions are presented as truth in the face of contradictory evidence.

Oversimplification of complex issues is another common characteristic of stupid answers. While simplification can be useful for explaining difficult concepts, oversimplification often leads to a distortion of reality. For example, reducing the complexities of international relations to simplistic notions of "good" and "evil" countries demonstrates a failure to grasp the nuanced interplay of historical, economic, and cultural factors that shape global politics.

Misunderstanding the question itself frequently results in stupid answers. This can occur when the respondent fails to grasp the context or intent behind the query. For instance, if asked about the ethical implications of artificial intelligence, a response focusing solely on the technical aspects of AI development would miss the mark entirely, demonstrating a failure to engage with the ethical dimension of the question.

Unfounded assumptions often form the basis of stupid answers, where the respondent leaps to conclusions without sufficient evidence or reasoning. This can be seen in conspiracy theories, where complex events are attributed to elaborate plots based on tenuous connections and speculation rather than factual analysis. Similarly, circular reasoning, where the conclusion is essentially restated as the premise, produces answers that offer no new information or insight. An example of this would be explaining the popularity of a product by saying, "It's popular because many people like it."

Lastly, stupid answers frequently have an **emotional** rather than rational basis. While emotions play an important role in human decision-making and understanding, answers that rely solely on emotional appeal without logical support often fall into the category of stupidity. For instance, rejecting a well-supported scientific theory simply because it makes one uncomfortable, without engaging with the evidence, exemplifies this emotional override of rational thought.

It's crucial to understand that even intelligent individuals can produce stupid answers due to various factors such as cognitive biases, lack of information, or momentary lapses in judgment. The key to avoiding stupid answers lies in cultivating critical thinking skills, maintaining an open mind to new information, and being willing to challenge one's own assumptions and beliefs. By recognizing the characteristics of stupid answers, we can work towards formulating more thoughtful, nuanced, and meaningful responses to the questions we encounter.

The Spectrum of Stupid Answers

The spectrum of stupid answers is a fascinating and complex phenomenon that spans a wide range of cognitive missteps and logical fallacies. At one end of this spectrum, we find mildly misguided responses that, while not entirely accurate, may contain kernels of truth or valid observations. These answers often stem from incomplete information or minor misconceptions rather than a fundamental lack of understanding. For instance, someone might claim that vitamin C cures the common cold. While this is not entirely accurate, as vitamin C cannot cure a viral infection, it does have some basis in truth since vitamin C can support the immune system and potentially reduce the duration of cold symptoms.

Moving further along the spectrum, we encounter significantly flawed answers that demonstrate more substantial misunderstandings or rely on faulty reasoning. These responses often involve logical fallacies or a misinterpretation of available evidence. An example of this might be the belief that vaccines cause autism. Despite overwhelming scientific evidence to the contrary, some individuals continue to hold this belief, often due to a misunderstanding of correlation versus causation or a mistrust of scientific institutions.

As we progress, we reach the realm of grossly incorrect answers that are fundamentally wrong and indicate a severe lack of understanding of the subject matter. These responses often arise from deeply ingrained misconceptions or a complete disregard for established facts. A prime example of this would be the flat Earth theory. Despite centuries of scientific evidence and direct observations that prove the Earth is spherical, proponents of this theory reject this fundamental fact, often constructing elaborate alternative explanations to support their beliefs.

At the far end of the spectrum lie the absurdly stupid answers, which are so divorced from reality or logic that they border on the nonsensical. These responses often defy not just established knowledge but also common sense and basic reasoning. An example of this might be the claim that the moon is made of cheese. This assertion is so patently absurd that it goes beyond mere misinformation and enters the realm of pure fantasy.

It's important to note that the placement of an answer on this spectrum can sometimes be subjective and context-dependent. What might seem absurdly stupid in one context could be merely misguided in another, depending on factors such as the age and education level of the respondent, cultural background, or the specific field of knowledge in question. For instance, a child's belief that thunder is caused by clouds bumping into each other might be considered mildly misguided, while the same belief held by an adult meteorologist would fall much further along the spectrum of stupidity.

Understanding this spectrum of stupid answers is crucial for several reasons. It allows us to approach flawed responses with appropriate levels of correction and education. Mildly misguided answers might require gentle correction and additional information, while absurdly stupid answers might necessitate a more fundamental reevaluation of the individual's thought processes and sources of information. Moreover, recognizing where our own answers might fall on this spectrum can help us cultivate intellectual humility and a willingness to revise our beliefs in the face of new evidence or better reasoning.

Art of Recognizing & Addressing Stupid Answer:

Developing critical thinking skills is essential for combating stupid answers. This process begins with questioning assumptions, a fundamental aspect of critical analysis. For instance, when presented with a statement like "Vaccines cause autism," one should examine the underlying assumptions, such as the presumed causal relationship between vaccination and autism spectrum disorders. Seeking evidence is equally crucial. In the case of the vaccine-autism claim, one would look for peer-reviewed scientific studies that have investigated this relationship, finding that extensive research has consistently debunked this notion.

Considering alternative explanations is another vital component of critical thinking. For example, if someone claims that a sudden increase in crime rates is solely due to immigration, a critical thinker would explore other potential factors such as economic conditions, changes in policing strategies, or shifts in demographic patterns. This approach helps to avoid simplistic, single-cause explanations for complex phenomena.

Recognizing bias, both in oneself and others, is a challenging but necessary skill. For instance, confirmation bias can lead people to selectively seek information that supports their preexisting beliefs while ignoring contradictory evidence. A person who believes in the efficacy of a particular diet might only pay attention to success stories while dismissing scientific studies that show its limitations or potential risks.

Fostering intellectual humility is crucial in preventing and addressing stupid answers. Acknowledging uncertainty is a key aspect of this. For example, in the rapidly evolving field of artificial intelligence, even experts often preface their predictions with caveats about the uncertainties involved in forecasting technological advancements. This approach contrasts sharply with those who make absolute claims about AI's future impact without acknowledging the complexities and unknowns in the field.

Embracing learning as a continuous process is another important aspect of intellectual humility. For instance, the field of medicine constantly evolves with new research and discoveries. A doctor who maintains intellectual humility would be open to updating their knowledge and practices based on new evidence, rather than stubbornly adhering to outdated methods.

Seeking diverse perspectives can significantly enhance one's understanding of complex issues. For example, in addressing global climate change, it's valuable to consider viewpoints from various stakeholders, including climate scientists, economists, policymakers, and representatives from different geographical regions and industries. This multifaceted approach can lead to more comprehensive and nuanced solutions.

Improving information literacy is crucial in an era of information overload. Evaluating sources is a key skill in this regard. For instance, when researching health information online, one should consider factors such as the credibility of the website (e.g., .gov or .edu domains), the qualifications of the authors, and whether the information is backed by scientific research.

Cross-referencing information from multiple reputable sources is another important aspect of information literacy. For example, when fact-checking a news story, one might compare reports from different respected news outlets, consult fact-checking websites, and look for primary sources of information.

Understanding media bias is crucial for navigating the modern information landscape. Different media outlets may frame the same event or issue in vastly different ways. For instance, coverage of economic policies might vary significantly between conservative and liberal-leaning news sources, emphasizing different aspects or interpretations of the same data.

Encouraging open dialogue is essential for combating stupid answers. Promoting constructive criticism involves creating an environment where ideas can be respectfully questioned and debated. In academic settings, for example, peer review processes exemplify this principle, allowing scholars to critically examine and improve each other's work.

Creating safe spaces for learning is about fostering environments where people feel comfortable admitting mistakes and learning from them. In a corporate setting, this might involve leaders openly discussing their own past errors and the lessons learned, thereby encouraging a culture of transparency and continuous improvement.

Rewarding intellectual curiosity can significantly contribute to combating stupid answers. This might involve encouraging employees to ask questions during meetings, even if they seem basic, or implementing programs that allow workers to explore areas outside their immediate job responsibilities.

Critical thinking skills can be applied to various real-world scenarios. For instance, when evaluating political campaign promises, one should question the assumptions behind proposed policies, seek evidence for their feasibility and potential impacts, consider alternative approaches, and recognize potential biases in how these promises are presented.

Intellectual humility plays a crucial role in scientific research. Scientists must be open to the possibility that their hypotheses might be wrong and be willing to revise their theories based on new evidence. The history of science is full of examples where long-held beliefs were overturned by new discoveries, such as the shift from Newtonian physics to Einstein's theory of relativity.

Information literacy skills are particularly important in the age of social media. For example, during election seasons, social media platforms are often flooded with political memes and infographics. A person with strong information literacy skills would know to verify the claims made in these posts by checking reputable news sources and fact-checking websites, rather than simply accepting and sharing them at face value.

The concept of media bias can be illustrated through the coverage of international conflicts. Different news outlets might emphasize different aspects of the conflict, use varying language to describe the parties involved, or give more airtime to certain perspectives. Recognizing these biases allows consumers of news to seek out multiple sources and form a more balanced understanding of complex geopolitical situations.

Open dialogue is particularly crucial in addressing societal issues. For instance, discussions about racial inequality benefit from creating spaces where people can share their experiences and perspectives without fear of judgment. This approach allows for a more nuanced understanding of the issue and can lead to more effective solutions.

The importance of questioning assumptions can be seen in the field of psychology. For many years, psychological research was predominantly conducted on WEIRD (Western, Educated, Industrialized, Rich, and Democratic) populations, leading to potentially biased conclusions about human behavior. Recognizing and questioning this assumption has led to more diverse and representative research in recent years.

Seeking evidence is particularly crucial in healthcare decisions. For example, when considering alternative medicine treatments, patients and healthcare providers should look for evidence from well-designed clinical trials rather than relying solely on anecdotal reports or traditional beliefs.

Considering alternative explanations is a valuable skill in criminal investigations. Detectives must avoid tunnel vision and consider multiple possible scenarios that could explain the evidence, rather than fixating on a single theory of the crime.

Recognizing bias is important in hiring processes. Unconscious biases can influence decisions about candidates, potentially leading to unfair outcomes. Many organizations now implement blind resume screening or structured interview processes to mitigate these biases.

Acknowledging uncertainty is crucial in fields like weather forecasting. Meteorologists often provide probability-based forecasts rather than absolute predictions, recognizing the inherent uncertainties in complex weather systems.

Embracing learning is essential in rapidly evolving fields like technology. Software developers, for instance, must continually update their skills and knowledge to keep pace with new programming languages, frameworks, and best practices.

Seeking diverse perspectives is valuable in product development. Companies that incorporate feedback from a diverse range of users are more likely to create products that meet the needs of a broader market. For example, early voice recognition systems often struggled with accents and dialects because they were primarily tested on a limited demographic.

Evaluating sources is crucial when researching health information online. Reputable sources like peer-reviewed medical journals, government health agencies, and respected medical institutions provide more reliable information than personal blogs or commercial websites with potential conflicts of interest.

Cross-referencing information is particularly important when fact-checking viral social media posts. Many fact-checking organizations use this technique, verifying claims against multiple reputable sources before determining their accuracy.

Understanding media bias is crucial when consuming news about complex scientific topics like climate change. Different outlets may emphasize different aspects of the issue, such as the economic impacts versus the environmental consequences, potentially influencing public perception and policy decisions.

Promoting constructive criticism is valuable in creative fields. In writing workshops, for instance, authors receive feedback from peers on their work, helping them identify areas for improvement and refine their craft.

Creating safe spaces for learning is important in educational settings. For example, some math teachers use "mistake-friendly" approaches, encouraging students to share and analyze their errors as a learning tool, rather than feeling ashamed of them.

Rewarding intellectual curiosity can drive innovation in businesses. Companies like Google have famously allowed employees to spend a portion of their work time on personal projects, leading to the development of products like Gmail and Google News.

Critical thinking skills are essential in personal finance decisions. When considering investment opportunities, individuals should question the assumptions behind promised returns, seek evidence of the investment's performance history, consider alternative investment options, and recognize potential biases in financial advice.

Intellectual humility is crucial in international diplomacy. Diplomats who approach negotiations with a willingness to learn about other cultures and perspectives are more likely to find mutually beneficial solutions to complex geopolitical issues.

Information literacy skills are vital in healthcare decision-making. Patients need to be able to understand and evaluate medical information to make informed decisions about their treatment options. This includes being able to interpret statistics about treatment efficacy and potential side effects.

Understanding media bias is important when consuming news about economic issues. Different news outlets may present the same economic data in vastly different ways, potentially influencing public opinion on economic policies.

Open dialogue is crucial in addressing environmental challenges. Effective solutions often require collaboration between scientists, policymakers, industry representatives, and community members, each bringing different perspectives and expertise to the table.

In conclusion, recognizing and addressing stupid answers requires a multifaceted approach that combines critical thinking, intellectual humility, information literacy, and open dialogue. By developing these skills and fostering environments that value them, we can improve the quality of discourse and decision-making across various domains of life and society.

Understanding how, why, and where answers can be stupid is crucial in our pursuit of knowledge and truth. By recognizing the factors that contribute to flawed answers, we can better equip ourselves to identify and address them. Moreover, this understanding can help us improve our own thinking and communication, leading to more accurate and insightful answers.

As we navigate an increasingly complex world, the ability to discern between quality information and "stupid" answers becomes ever more critical. By developing our critical thinking skills, fostering intellectual humility, improving our information literacy, and encouraging open dialogue, we can create a society that is more resistant to the spread of misinformation and flawed reasoning.

Ultimately, the goal is not to ridicule or dismiss those who provide stupid answers, but to create an environment where everyone is empowered to think more critically and communicate more effectively. In doing so, we can elevate the quality of our collective knowledge and decision-making, leading to better outcomes in all areas of life.

CHAPTER SIX

The Art of Deep Listening and Questioning

In our fast-paced, information-saturated world, the ability to truly listen and ask meaningful questions has become an increasingly rare and valuable skill. The art of deep listening and questioning is not merely about hearing words or formulating inquiries; it's about cultivating a profound level of understanding, empathy, and insight that can transform our personal and professional relationships.

Deep listening involves fully engaging with the speaker, absorbing not just their words but also their tone, body language, and underlying emotions. It requires setting aside our own preconceptions and judgments to create a space where genuine communication can flourish. This practice goes beyond passive reception; it's an active process that demands our full attention and presence.

Complementing deep listening is the skill of asking thoughtful, probing questions. These questions serve to clarify, expand, and deepen our understanding of the speaker's perspective. They can uncover hidden assumptions, reveal new insights, and guide conversations towards more meaningful and productive outcomes.

Together, these interconnected skills form a powerful tool for enhancing communication, fostering empathy, and promoting mutual understanding. Whether in personal relationships, professional settings, or broader social contexts, mastering the art of deep listening and questioning can lead to more authentic connections, innovative problem-solving, and personal growth.

In the following sections, we will explore the principles, techniques, and benefits of deep listening and questioning, providing practical strategies to develop and refine these essential skills.

Are we Hearing or Listening: The Science of Hearing

Hearing is a physiological process that involves the perception of sound. Sound waves enter the ear canal, causing the eardrum to vibrate. These vibrations are then transmitted through the middle ear bones to the cochlea in the inner ear, where they are converted into electrical signals that the brain interprets as sound.

While hearing is a passive process that happens automatically, listening is an active process that requires conscious effort and engagement.

Defining Active Listening

Active listening is the practice of fully concentrating on, understanding, responding to, and remembering what is being said. It involves not just the ears, but the mind and often the body as well. Active listeners engage with the speaker, provide feedback, and demonstrate their attentiveness through both verbal and non-verbal cues.

The Importance of Active Listening

Active listening is a fundamental skill that plays a crucial role in various aspects of life, profoundly impacting our personal relationships, professional endeavors, educational experiences, and conflict resolution abilities. In personal relationships, active listening serves as the cornerstone for building and maintaining strong, meaningful connections. By fully engaging with our partners, friends, and family members, we demonstrate genuine interest and care, fostering a deep sense of understanding and empathy. This practice allows us to truly comprehend the thoughts, feelings, and needs of our loved ones, creating an environment of trust and emotional intimacy. For instance, when a friend shares a personal struggle, active listening enables us to offer support that is truly aligned with their needs, rather than making assumptions or offering generic advice.

In professional settings, the importance of active listening cannot be overstated. It serves as a catalyst for improved communication, which is essential for the smooth operation of any organization. By attentively listening to colleagues, clients, and superiors, we can grasp nuances in instructions, understand project requirements more accurately, and pick up on subtle cues that might otherwise be missed. This heightened level of comprehension significantly reduces the likelihood of errors and misunderstandings, leading to enhanced productivity and efficiency. For example, in a team meeting, an active listener might pick up on an underlying concern that a colleague is hesitant to express directly, allowing for proactive problem-solving and potentially averting future issues.

The educational sphere is another domain where active listening proves invaluable. Students who practice active listening are better equipped to absorb and retain information, leading to improved academic performance. By fully engaging with lectures, discussions, and explanations, learners can process information more effectively, make connections between different concepts, and ask more insightful questions. This deeper level of engagement not only enhances immediate comprehension but also promotes long-term retention of knowledge. For instance, a student actively listening in a history class might draw parallels between past events and current affairs, leading to a richer understanding of both historical and contemporary contexts.

In the realm of conflict resolution, active listening emerges as a powerful tool for bridging divides and finding common ground. When parties in conflict truly listen to each other, they gain insight into the underlying motivations, fears, and needs driving the disagreement. This understanding is crucial for moving beyond surface-level disputes and addressing the root causes of conflict. Active listening in these situations involves not just hearing the words spoken but also paying attention to tone, body language, and emotional subtext. For example, in a workplace dispute, an active listener might recognize that a colleague's aggressive stance stems from feeling undervalued, allowing for a resolution that addresses this underlying issue rather than just the immediate conflict.

Moreover, active listening contributes significantly to personal growth and self-awareness. By attentively listening to others, we often gain new perspectives and insights that challenge our own assumptions and beliefs. This process of exposure to diverse viewpoints can broaden our understanding of the world and foster intellectual and emotional growth. Additionally, the practice of active listening can help us become more aware of our own thought patterns and biases, leading to greater self-reflection and personal development.

In leadership roles, active listening is a critical skill that can dramatically enhance one's effectiveness. Leaders who are adept at active listening are better able to understand the needs and concerns of their team members, fostering a sense of trust and respect. This, in turn, can lead to increased employee engagement, higher morale, and improved overall performance. For instance, a manager who actively listens during performance reviews might uncover underlying factors affecting an employee's work that were not immediately apparent, allowing for more targeted and effective support.

The practice of active listening also plays a vital role in customer service and client relations. Service providers who excel in active listening can more accurately identify customer needs, address concerns effectively, and provide solutions that truly meet the client's requirements. This level of attentiveness not only leads to higher customer satisfaction but can also result in increased customer loyalty and positive word-of-mouth referrals.

In the field of healthcare, active listening is an essential component of effective patient care. Healthcare providers who practice active listening can gather more comprehensive patient histories, pick up on subtle symptoms or concerns that patients might be hesitant to express directly, and build stronger therapeutic relationships. This can lead to more accurate diagnoses, better treatment adherence, and improved patient outcomes.

In conclusion, active listening is a multifaceted skill that permeates every aspect of our lives, from our most intimate personal relationships to our professional interactions and beyond. Its importance lies not just in the immediate benefits of improved communication and understanding, but in its power to foster deeper connections, drive personal and professional growth, and create more harmonious and productive environments in all areas of life. By cultivating and prioritizing active listening, we open ourselves to a richer, more nuanced understanding of the world around us and the people in it, paving the way for more meaningful interactions and more effective problem-solving in all spheres of life.

Let's develop Active and Deep Listening

Deep listening is a fundamental skill that goes beyond merely hearing words; it involves a profound level of engagement and understanding. This practice requires cultivating a heightened awareness of not only the spoken words but also the underlying emotions, intentions, and context of the speaker. By developing deep listening skills, individuals can foster stronger relationships, improve communication, and gain deeper insights into others' perspectives.

At its core, deep listening involves creating a space of receptivity and openness. This means setting aside one's own thoughts, judgments, and preconceptions to fully focus on the speaker. It requires a willingness to be present in the moment, allowing oneself to be fully immersed in the conversation without the distraction of formulating responses or thinking about unrelated matters.

One of the key aspects of deep listening is the cultivation of empathy. This involves not only understanding the literal meaning of the words being spoken but also attempting to grasp the emotional state and perspective of the speaker. By doing so, the listener can create a sense of connection and trust, encouraging the speaker to share more openly and authentically.

Practicing deep listening also involves paying attention to non-verbal cues. Body language, tone of voice, and facial expressions can often convey as much, if not more, than the words themselves. By attuning oneself to these subtle signals, the listener can gain a more comprehensive understanding of the speaker's message and emotional state.

Another crucial aspect of deep listening is the ability to manage one's own internal dialogue. This involves recognizing when the mind begins to wander or when personal biases and assumptions start to influence the interpretation of what is being said. By consciously bringing attention back to the speaker and suspending judgment, the listener can maintain a more objective and open-minded stance.

Developing deep listening skills requires practice and patience. It involves cultivating mindfulness and self-awareness, as well as a genuine curiosity about others' perspectives. By consistently applying techniques such as paraphrasing to confirm understanding, asking clarifying questions, and providing non-verbal cues of engagement, individuals can gradually enhance their capacity for deep listening.

The benefits of mastering deep listening are numerous. It can lead to improved relationships, both personal and professional, as others feel truly heard and understood. In the workplace, deep listening can enhance collaboration, problem-solving, and decision-making by ensuring that all perspectives are fully considered. On a personal level, it can foster empathy, compassion, and a greater sense of connection with others.

In conclusion, developing deep listening skills is a transformative process that can significantly enhance one's ability to communicate effectively and build meaningful relationships. By cultivating presence, empathy, and self-awareness, individuals can create a space for authentic and profound interactions, leading to greater understanding and connection in all areas of life.

Understanding Questions and Absorption of Context

Understanding questions and absorbing context are crucial skills in effective communication and learning. These abilities enable individuals to grasp the full meaning of inquiries and comprehend the surrounding circumstances, leading to more insightful responses and deeper understanding.

Questions are powerful tools that serve multiple purposes beyond simply seeking information. They can stimulate critical thinking, challenge assumptions, and inspire creativity. When we encounter a question, it's essential to analyze not just its literal meaning but also its underlying intent and implications. This deeper understanding allows us to provide more comprehensive and relevant answers.

For example, consider the question, "What are the main causes of climate change?" On the surface, this may seem like a straightforward request for a list of factors. However, a deeper analysis might reveal that the questioner is seeking to understand the complex interplay between human activities and natural processes, the relative impact of different factors, and potentially the historical context of climate change.

Absorption of context goes hand in hand with understanding questions. It involves taking in and processing all the relevant information surrounding a topic or situation. This includes not only the explicit details provided but also implicit information, cultural nuances, and historical background. By absorbing context, we can form a more holistic understanding of the subject matter.

For instance, when discussing the impact of a new technology, absorbing context might involve considering factors such as:

1. The current state of the industry
2. Societal trends and values
3. Regulatory environment
4. Potential ethical implications
5. Historical precedents of similar technological advancements

By considering these contextual elements, one can provide a more nuanced and comprehensive analysis of the technology's potential impact.

Improving our ability to understand questions and absorb context requires active engagement and practice. One effective technique is to regularly ask clarifying questions to ensure a complete understanding of the inquiry or situation. This might involve rephrasing the question in your own words or asking for specific examples to illustrate the point.

Another useful approach is to consciously seek out diverse perspectives on a topic. This can help broaden our understanding of the context and reveal aspects we might not have considered initially. For example, when examining a historical event, consulting sources from different cultural backgrounds or time periods can provide a more comprehensive view of its significance and impact.

Visualization techniques can also aid in the absorption of context. Creating mental maps or diagrams that illustrate the relationships between different elements of a situation can help organize and retain complex information. For instance, when studying the causes and effects of a major historical event, creating a visual timeline or cause-and-effect diagram can help clarify the connections between various factors.

Moreover, actively engaging with the material through discussions, debates, or teaching others can significantly enhance our understanding and absorption of context. Explaining concepts to others often requires us to reorganize and clarify our own thoughts, leading to deeper comprehension.

In conclusion, developing the skills to understand questions deeply and absorb context effectively is a continuous process that requires practice and conscious effort. By honing these abilities, we can enhance our capacity for critical thinking, improve our communication skills, and gain a more nuanced understanding of complex topics and situations. This, in turn, enables us to engage more meaningfully in discussions, make more informed decisions, and contribute more valuable insights in both personal and professional contexts.

The Interplay of Listening, Questioning, and Absorbing

The process of effective communication and learning is a dynamic interplay between listening, questioning, and absorbing information. These three elements work in harmony, creating a virtuous cycle that enhances understanding, promotes deeper engagement, and facilitates meaningful exchanges of ideas.

At the foundation of this interplay is deep listening. When we truly listen, we open ourselves to the full spectrum of information being conveyed, both verbally and non-verbally. This attentive listening allows us to grasp not only the content of what's being said but also the underlying emotions, motivations, and context. For instance, in a business meeting, deep listening might involve not just hearing a colleague's proposal, but also noting their tone of voice, body language, and the reactions of others in the room.

As we listen deeply, we naturally begin to formulate questions. These questions arise from our genuine curiosity and desire to understand more fully. They are not mere interruptions or attempts to showcase our own knowledge, but rather thoughtful inquiries that seek to clarify, expand, or explore the topic at hand. For example, after listening to a presentation on a new marketing strategy, one might ask, "How does this approach align with our company's long-term goals?" or "What potential challenges do you foresee in implementing this strategy?"

The act of questioning serves multiple purposes. It helps to fill gaps in our understanding, challenges assumptions, and often leads the conversation in new and insightful directions. Moreover, the process of formulating and asking questions engages our critical thinking skills, allowing us to interact more meaningfully with the information we're receiving.

As we receive answers to our questions and continue to listen attentively, we begin to absorb the information more effectively. This absorption goes beyond mere memorization; it involves integrating new knowledge with our existing understanding, making connections, and applying insights to different contexts. For instance, a student learning about historical events might absorb the information by relating it to current global issues or by drawing parallels with personal experiences.

The beauty of this interplay lies in its cyclical nature. As we absorb information, our capacity for deep listening is enhanced. We develop a more nuanced understanding of the subject matter, which in turn allows us to ask even more insightful questions. These questions lead to more valuable information, creating a self-reinforcing cycle of learning and understanding.

Consider a scenario where a mentor is guiding a mentee through a complex project. The mentee listens carefully as the mentor explains the project's objectives and challenges. This deep listening enables the mentee to ask pertinent questions about specific aspects of the project. The mentor's responses provide valuable insights, which the mentee absorbs and integrates into their understanding. This enhanced understanding then allows the mentee to listen even more effectively in subsequent discussions, ask more sophisticated questions, and absorb information at a deeper level.

This virtuous cycle of listening, questioning, and absorbing is not limited to formal learning environments. It plays out in everyday conversations, professional settings, and personal relationships. By consciously engaging in this interplay, we can enhance our communication skills, deepen our understanding of various subjects, and foster more meaningful connections with others.

In conclusion, the interplay of listening, questioning, and absorbing is a powerful tool for personal and professional growth. By cultivating these skills and recognizing their interconnected nature, we can become more effective communicators, learners, and problem-solvers. This dynamic process enables us to engage more deeply with the world around us, continuously expanding our knowledge and understanding.

The Ethics of Listening and Questioning

The practice of deep listening and thoughtful questioning is not only a skill but also an ethical responsibility. As we engage in conversations, whether personal or professional, we must be mindful of the profound impact our listening and questioning can have on others. This ethical dimension encompasses various aspects, including privacy, consent, responsibility, and power dynamics.

Privacy and consent form the cornerstone of ethical listening and questioning. In our increasingly interconnected world, where information is often freely shared, it's crucial to recognize and respect personal boundaries. Before delving into sensitive topics or asking probing questions, one should always consider whether it's appropriate to do so and seek explicit or implicit consent from the speaker. For example, in a professional setting, a manager discussing an employee's performance should be cautious about inquiring into personal matters that may not directly relate to work. Similarly, in personal relationships, friends should be attuned to non-verbal cues that might indicate discomfort with certain topics, respecting the other person's right to privacy.

The responsibility of the listener extends beyond mere attentiveness; it involves a commitment to handle shared information with care and respect. When someone opens up and shares personal or sensitive information, they are placing their trust in the listener. This trust carries an implicit expectation that the information will be treated confidentially and with empathy. For instance, if a colleague confides about workplace challenges they're facing, it would be unethical to gossip about this information with other coworkers. Instead, the ethical listener should offer support and maintain confidentiality unless explicitly given permission to share.

An often overlooked aspect of the ethics of listening and questioning is the power dynamics at play in various communication contexts. In many situations, the act of questioning can be a form of control or manipulation, especially when there's an imbalance of power between the parties involved. This is particularly evident in settings such as job interviews, police interrogations, or even in certain personal relationships. For example, a teacher questioning a student should be aware of how their authority might influence the student's responses and should strive to create a safe, non-threatening environment for open dialogue.

It's also important to consider the intent behind our questions. Are we asking to genuinely understand and support, or are we seeking information to gain an advantage or satisfy our curiosity at the expense of the other person's comfort? Ethical questioning involves being mindful of our motivations and the potential impact of our inquiries on others.

Moreover, the ethics of listening and questioning extend to how we process and act upon the information we receive. Active listening involves not just hearing words but also understanding context and emotions. It requires us to suspend judgment and approach the conversation with an open mind. For instance, when listening to a friend share their struggles, it would be unethical to dismiss their feelings or immediately jump to offering solutions without fully understanding their perspective.

In professional settings, such as journalism or research, the ethics of listening and questioning take on additional dimensions. Journalists must balance their duty to inform the public with respect for individuals' privacy and the potential consequences of their reporting. Researchers conducting interviews or surveys must adhere to strict ethical guidelines to protect participants' rights and well-being.

Ultimately, ethical listening and questioning are about creating a safe, respectful space for communication. It involves being aware of our own biases, respecting boundaries, and using our skills to foster understanding rather than to manipulate or control. By approaching conversations with empathy, integrity, and awareness of power dynamics, we can engage in more meaningful and ethical interactions, building trust and deepening our connections with others.

Towards conclusion of this section, its worth mentioning that in a world of constant noise and distraction, the ability to truly listen, to ask insightful questions, and to deeply absorb information is more valuable than ever. By developing these skills, we can enhance our understanding, improve our relationships, and navigate the complexities of modern life more effectively. Remember, communication is not just about being heard, but about hearing others. It's not just about asking questions, but about understanding the answers. And it's not just about absorbing information, but about integrating it into our understanding of the world. By mastering the art of deep listening and questioning, we open ourselves to a richer, more nuanced experience of life and human connection.

CHAPTER SEVEN

Understanding the Intent: The Key to Effective Communication

Communication is far more than a simple exchange of words; it's a complex interplay of intentions, emotions, and interpretations. At the heart of truly effective communication lies a crucial skill: the ability to understand intent. This chapter delves into the pivotal role that grasping the underlying purpose and motivation behind messages plays in fostering clear, meaningful, and productive interactions.

In our daily lives, we engage in countless conversations, each with its own unique context and purpose. Whether in personal relationships, professional settings, or casual encounters, the intent behind our words often carries more weight than the words themselves. Misunderstandings frequently arise not from what is said, but from a failure to recognize the true intention behind the communication.

Understanding intent requires a combination of keen observation, active listening, and emotional intelligence. It involves looking beyond the surface level of words to discern the deeper motivations, needs, and desires that drive communication. This skill is not just about decoding messages; it's about connecting with the essence of what others are trying to convey.

As we explore this topic, we'll examine various aspects of intent in communication, including:

- The role of context in shaping intent
- Non-verbal cues that reveal underlying motivations
- Common barriers to understanding intent
- Techniques for improving intent recognition

- The impact of cultural differences on interpreting intent

By honing our ability to understand intent, we can dramatically improve the quality of our interactions, reduce misunderstandings, and build stronger, more empathetic relationships. This chapter aims to equip you with the knowledge and tools necessary to become a more perceptive and effective communicator, capable of navigating the complex landscape of human interaction with greater ease and insight.

The Nature of Questions and Intent

Questions are not always straightforward requests for information. Often, they carry hidden meanings, emotions, and motivations that go beyond their surface-level content. To truly understand and respond effectively, we must learn to decode the intent behind the questions we encounter.

Types of Questions and Their Underlying Intents

Questions are powerful tools in communication, serving various purposes beyond mere information gathering. Understanding the different types of questions and their underlying intents can significantly enhance our ability to navigate conversations effectively and build stronger relationships.

Introductory questions, often simple and seemingly casual, play a crucial role in initiating dialogue and setting the tone for further interaction. When someone asks, "How's work going?" or "What have you been up to lately?", their intent typically extends beyond a literal inquiry about your professional life or recent activities. These questions serve as social lubricants, designed to break the ice and create an opening for more substantive conversation. The underlying intent is to establish a connection, show interest in the other person's life, and pave the way for deeper engagement.

Mirror questions, a common response to introductory queries, reflect an important aspect of social dynamics. When someone responds to your question with a similar one, such as replying "Good, how about you?" to your inquiry about their well-being, they're engaging in a form of conversational reciprocity. This type of question serves multiple intents: it maintains balance in the interaction, demonstrates mutual interest, and adheres to social norms of politeness. By mirroring the question, the respondent also keeps the conversation open-ended, allowing for further exploration of topics that either party might want to discuss.

Full-switch questions represent a more assertive approach to steering conversations. When someone abruptly changes the subject with a question like "Did you watch the game last night?", their intent could be multifaceted. They might be attempting to move the conversation to a topic they find more engaging or comfortable. Alternatively, they could be trying to avoid a potentially sensitive or uncomfortable subject that the previous line of conversation was approaching. In some cases, full-switch questions can also be used to include others in a group conversation by introducing a topic of common interest.

Follow-up questions are perhaps the most potent tools for deepening conversations and demonstrating genuine interest. When someone asks, "What are you working on at the moment?" after you've mentioned your job, they're showing active engagement with what you've said. The intent behind follow-up questions is often to gain a more comprehensive understanding of the topic at hand, to show empathy or support, or to find common ground. These questions can also serve to validate the speaker's experiences or opinions, making them feel heard and valued.

Understanding these different types of questions and their intents can significantly enhance our communication skills. By recognizing the purpose behind a question, we can respond more appropriately, engage more meaningfully in conversations, and build stronger connections with others. Moreover, being aware of these question types allows us to use them more effectively in our own communication, helping us to navigate social situations with greater ease and achieve our conversational goals more successfully.

Decoding Intent: CROR analogy

The CROR (**Content, Reason, Outcome, Reflection**) framework is a practical tool for decoding the intent behind questions and formulating effective responses. This systematic approach helps communicators analyze and address the underlying motivations and goals of the questioner, leading to more meaningful and productive interactions.

Content, the first element of the framework, focuses on the specific information being sought. It requires careful analysis of the question's structure and wording to determine whether it's open-ended or closed, and what particular data or insights are being requested. For example, a manager asking "How is the project progressing?" is seeking a general update, while

"What specific challenges are delaying the project timeline?" aims for more detailed information about obstacles.

The Reason behind a question delves into the questioner's motivation. Understanding why a question is being asked provides valuable context for formulating an appropriate response. For instance, a team member asking "Why did we choose this approach?" could be seeking clarification to better understand the process, or they might be subtly challenging the decision. Recognizing the underlying reason allows for a more tailored and effective answer.

Outcome refers to the questioner's desired result from asking the question. This aspect of the framework encourages consideration of what the person hopes to achieve. A colleague inquiring "What do you think about the new marketing strategy?" might be looking to gather diverse opinions, build consensus, or potentially sway others to their point of view. Identifying the intended outcome helps in framing a response that addresses not just the literal question, but also the questioner's broader goals.

The Reflection component of CROR prompts consideration of the question's potential impact on the conversation or situation. It involves anticipating how the question and its answer might shape the direction of the discussion or influence relationships. For example, a team leader asking "Who's responsible for this mistake?" in a group setting could create tension or defensiveness. Recognizing this potential impact allows for a more thoughtful and constructive response that addresses the issue without escalating conflict.

By systematically applying the CROR framework, communicators can develop a more nuanced understanding of questions and their underlying intents. This approach enables more effective responses that address not only the surface-level inquiry but also the deeper motivations and desired outcomes of the questioner. As a result, conversations become more productive, misunderstandings are reduced, and relationships are strengthened through improved mutual understanding and more targeted communication.

Navigating the Challenging Conversions

Navigating challenging conversations is a crucial skill in both personal and professional settings. When faced with difficult or confrontational questions, the ability to discern and address the underlying intent becomes even more critical. These situations often arise unexpectedly and can be emotionally charged, making it essential to have strategies in place to handle them effectively.

One of the most valuable strategies in managing challenging conversations is the practice of pausing and reflecting before responding. This brief moment of contemplation allows you to process the question, consider its implications, and formulate a thoughtful response. For example, if a colleague abruptly questions your decision-making in a project, taking a deep breath and a short pause can help you avoid a defensive reaction and instead respond with clarity and professionalism.

Seeking clarification is another powerful tool when navigating difficult conversations. If the intent behind a question is unclear or seems loaded with hidden meaning, it's often beneficial to ask follow-up questions. This approach not only helps you gain a better understanding of the questioner's concerns but also demonstrates your willingness to engage in a meaningful dialogue. For instance, if a team member asks, "Why are we wasting time on this approach?" instead of becoming defensive, you might respond with, "Can you help me understand your specific concerns about this approach?".

Acknowledging emotions is a critical aspect of handling challenging questions. Often, the emotional content of a question can be more significant than the literal words used. By recognizing and addressing these emotions, you can create a more empathetic and productive conversation. For example, if a client angrily asks why a project is behind schedule, you might respond by saying, "I understand your frustration with the delay. Let's discuss the specific issues and how we can address them to get back on track." This approach acknowledges the emotional aspect while steering the conversation towards problem-solving.

Reframing is a powerful technique that can transform a confrontational question into an opportunity for constructive dialogue. By reframing, you can address the underlying concern more effectively and shift the conversation in a more positive direction. For instance, if an employee asks, "Why don't you trust me to handle this project?" you might reframe the question by responding, "I'm glad you're interested in taking on more responsibility. Let's discuss how we can work together to build your skills in this area."

In addition to these strategies, it's important to maintain a calm and composed demeanor throughout challenging conversations. Your body language, tone of voice, and facial expressions can significantly impact the direction and outcome of the interaction. By remaining calm and focused, you can help de-escalate tense situations and guide the conversation towards a productive resolution.

It's also crucial to remember that challenging conversations often stem from genuine concerns or unmet needs. By approaching these interactions with empathy and a willingness to understand, you can often uncover valuable insights and strengthen relationships. For example, a team member's confrontational questions about a new policy might reveal important considerations that were overlooked in its development.

Practicing active listening is another key component in navigating difficult conversations. By giving your full attention to the speaker, paraphrasing their concerns, and asking thoughtful questions, you demonstrate respect and a genuine desire to understand their perspective. This approach can often diffuse tension and pave the way for more collaborative problem-solving.

In conclusion, navigating challenging conversations requires a combination of self-awareness, empathy, and strategic communication skills. By employing strategies such as pausing to reflect, seeking clarification, acknowledging emotions, and reframing questions, you can transform potentially confrontational interactions into opportunities for growth, understanding, and improved relationships. Remember that with practice and patience, these skills can be developed and refined, enabling you to handle even the most difficult conversations with confidence and grace.

By shifting our focus from merely answering questions to addressing the underlying intent, we open up new possibilities for meaningful, empathetic, and effective communication. This approach not only enhances our personal and professional relationships but also contributes to a more understanding and connected society as a whole.

As we continue to practice and refine our ability to discern and respond to intent, we'll find that our conversations become richer, our relationships deeper, and our impact on others more profound. The journey towards mastering this skill is ongoing, but the rewards—in terms of improved understanding, stronger connections, and more satisfying interactions—are immeasurable.

CHAPTER EIGHT

Conclusion: The Power of Questions and Answers in Shaping Our World

As we reach the end of our exploration into the art of questioning and answering, it's clear that these fundamental human activities are far more than mere exchanges of information. They are the building blocks of knowledge, the catalysts for innovation, and the bridges that connect us in understanding and empathy.

Throughout this book, we've journeyed through the universal art of inquiry, examining how different cultures have approached the practice of questioning. We've seen how the right questions can lead to profound insights and how the nature of our answers reflects not just our knowledge, but our thought processes and biases.

We've delved into the anatomy of stupidity, dissecting flawed answers to understand the cognitive pitfalls and logical fallacies that can lead us astray. This exploration has highlighted the importance of critical thinking and the need for intellectual humility in our quest for knowledge.

The art of deep listening and questioning has emerged as a powerful tool for enhancing communication and fostering genuine understanding. We've learned that truly hearing others and asking thoughtful questions can transform our personal and professional relationships, leading to more meaningful connections and innovative problem-solving.

As we look to the future, the importance of effective questioning and answering in our digital age becomes ever more apparent. In a world awash with information, the ability to ask incisive questions, critically evaluate answers, and engage in deep, meaningful dialogue is more crucial than ever.

The journey we've undertaken in this book is not just an academic exercise. It's a call to action – an invitation to cultivate curiosity, embrace critical thinking, and engage more deeply with the world around us. By honing our skills in questioning and answering, we equip ourselves to navigate the complexities of modern life, to challenge assumptions, and to drive progress in all fields of human endeavor.

As we close this chapter, let us remember that every question we ask and every answer we give has the potential to shape our understanding, influence our decisions, and impact our world. The power of questions and answers lies not just in the information they convey, but in their ability to inspire, to challenge, and to transform.

May this book serve as a guide and inspiration in your ongoing journey of inquiry and discovery. As you move forward, carry with you the lessons learned here – the importance of asking the right questions, the value of listening deeply, and the transformative power of thoughtful, well-reasoned answers.

Remember, the greatest questions are those that lead not to final answers, but to even more profound questions. In this endless cycle of inquiry and discovery lies the true essence of human progress and understanding. So go forth, question boldly, listen deeply, and answer thoughtfully. For in doing so, you contribute to the grand dialogue of human knowledge and understanding that has propelled our species forward since time immemorial.

The journey of questioning and answering is never truly complete. It is a lifelong adventure, full of wonder, challenge, and discovery. Embrace it with an open mind and a curious heart, and you will find that the world is full of mysteries waiting to be unraveled, insights waiting to be uncovered, and connections waiting to be made.

As you close this book, consider the questions it has sparked in your mind and the answers it has challenged you to reconsider. Let these be the starting points for your own explorations, your own questioning, and your own journey of discovery. For in the end, it is not the answers we find, but the questions we ask that truly define us and shape our world.

www.ingramcontent.com/pod-product-compliance
Lightning Source LLC
La Vergne TN
LVHW041120150826
845673LV00007B/2135

* 9 7 9 8 8 9 5 8 8 5 6 0 4 *